THIS BOOK IS FOR DEMELZA

Front cover:
English Champion Graecia Mercury - (A. & M. Rostron)

Back cover:
Australian Champion Gameguard Bruelle - (Ernie & Glenn Spareham)

Contents page: Courtney's Pride Pup (J. Frijling)

Title page: Canadian Ch Garroway's Good Thunder (S. DaSilva)

This page: Courtney's Pride Pups (J. Frijling)

Aus & NZ Ch Gameguard Yukon
handled by Rebecca Dalglish

Opalguard Robbie (Photo courtesy N. Marshall)

PREFACE

It occurred to me many years ago that the uniqueness of the Bullmastiff was lost in the generality of other bull breeds and often, incorrectly, it was grouped with them in respect to psychology, temperament and disposition.
This love affair with the breed took me to many Bullmastiff kennels in the United States, Canada, Finland Sweden, Australia, New Zealand and Britain, and I asked questions wherever I went. What I learned over these many years, and the experience gained from it, is the basis of the information found in this book. There is a look that says 'This is a Bullmastiff'; a look you will never forget, that stirs you from within. If that look is not there, it is not a good Bullmastiff...or maybe is another breed.
Thanks to Joy, Nicola ,Shane, and not forgetting Janice Swan whose help and understanding brought this about, without whom, I would not be writing here today. Special thanks to Riikka Holappa from Finland who has supported me over all these years and sent me such superb pictures for this book - thank you, Riikka!

Bill Walkey

FOREWORD

I have known Bill Walkey for a good number of years during which time I have found him to be very knowledgeable, not only of this magnificent breed but also many others. He is approved to judge many breeds at championship level by the canine controlling bodies of the vast majority of countries throughout the world. Bill is a true dog man having bred and

campaigned dogs to champions in various breeds.
As a fellow author, judge and lover of the bullmastiff with more than 55 years experience of the breed I greatly appreciate the opportunity to write the foreword for this work by such a renowned author, a man for whom I have a high regard. This book is a sequel of the author's previous bullmastiff books and as such it is well researched and written to the same high standard as those previous much read books. These books are without doubt comprehensive, coverering all aspects appertaining to the bullmastiff.

The modern bullmastiff is truly a man made breed developed from the gamekeepers' nightdogs, the purpose of which was to protect the gamekeepers from the very real life threatening menace posed by poachers and their dogs.
I believe that due to the restrictions associated with travel several other breeds were used in those early days to produce a desired type of dog. One must bear in mind that travel was extremely difficult in those times and therefore it was not uncommon for gamekeepers to use any suitable breeding animal that was within a reasonable travelling distance.
As can be seen the requirements for such a breed are for a medium sized working dog with stamina and tenacity, one that has balanced construction, is powerfully built, in hard muscular condition, fit, agile and completely biddable. These attributes are equally essential today as they were then together with all those desired to fit into the breeds' new role that of family pet and companion.

Although the true origins of the nightdogs are lost in the annals of history the origins of the modern day bullmastiff are accredited to men such as Mr Burton(Thorneywood), J Biggs (Osmaston), J Barnard and S E Mosley (Farcroft). These stalwarts worked with crosses between the mastiff and the old type bulldog commonly referred to as the "Butchers Dog".

From the novice to the more experienced all will find the information contained within these pages extremely helpful. All those interested in this noble and majestic breed should make it their business to have this book in their bookcase. No collection of bullmastiff literature should be considered as complete without it.

Alan Rostron (Graecia Bullmastiffs): England

INTRODUCTION

The names Bullmastiff, Bull and Mastiff, Bandog, Tiedog and Gamekeeper's Night Dog have created an identity confusion of the breed known today as the Bullmastiff. It is one of the few dogs that was not adopted by Royalty and hence has not enjoyed the promotional publicity enjoyed by such breeds.

Owing to this, its origins, purposes and history have become a little obscure over time and lost in the annals of history. In the 1930s, breed historians such as Eric Makins and Arthur Craven did their best to acquaint the public with the breed of that time.

This book provides background, methods and a 'how-to' for novices and first-time owners, plus a host of information for the long-time fancier, in a comprehensive format to supplement the true fancier's library.

Int. No. Se. Fin. Ch Rambull's Lily Of The Valley (Photo courtesy Mary Heli)

CONTENTS

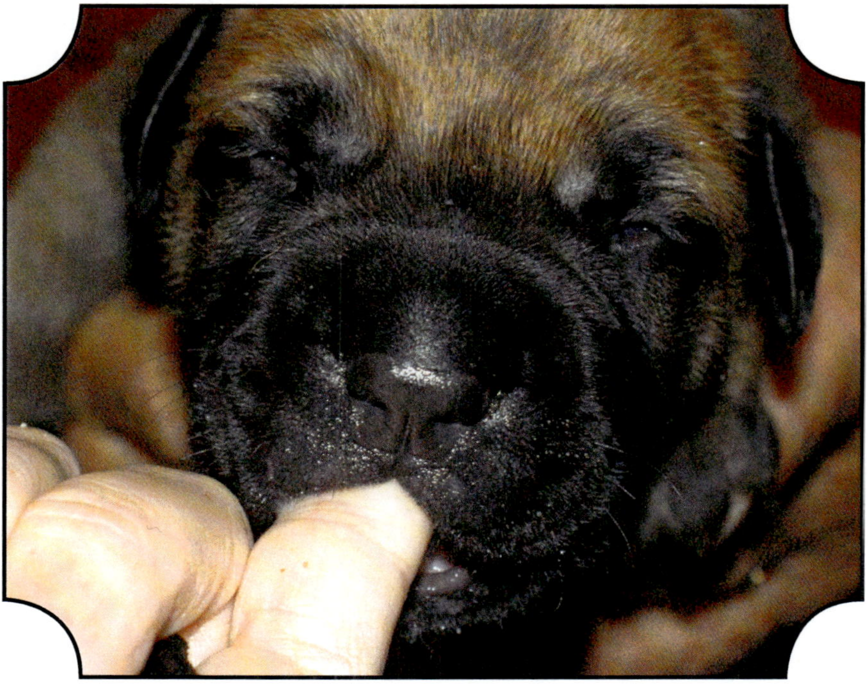

CHAPTER ONE

Introduction to the Breed

Murbisa's Chance (Photo courtesy of M. & J. Bissat)

Aus Ch OnDuty Lockstocknbarrel (Photo: K & G Manlein)

So, you've decided to add a special member to your family but are not sure which breed to choose. Well, let me tell you about a special dog: the Bullmastiff. He is large: at 0.75m (2ft) high at the shoulder and 58kg (130lb) in weight, he is an ominous deterrent to intruders. To his family, however, he is a big, soft, loving pet. He is gentle with his loved ones and does not take up as much room in the house as his appearance first suggests. He is quiet, not usually barking unless there is a problem he cannot investigate; then he barks to warn you of the problem.

The Bullmastiff's coat is waterproof, so he can thrive when kept outside in a sheltered kennel. The breed was originally developed to guard estates, so your garden must be fenced to give him his (your) estate boundaries; the neighbours may not appreciate your dog claiming their gardens as his private property! A Bullmastiff is too heavy to jump over fences; he jumps against them. To avoid a collapsed fence it is a good idea to have a rail about 1.5m (5ft) off the ground on your fence for him to jump against.

The Bullmastiff will be naturally defensive of his own territory, so gates at all points of access should be secure. There is nothing more upsetting to an unsuspecting acquaintance entering your property for a friendly visit than to find a Bullmastiff coming to investigate him at full speed. On the positive side, the Bullmastiff is a knock-down-and-pin dog, not a biter, so your guest may feel a little indignant but will come to no harm as long as he does not retaliate.

If he does, the dog will stand no nonsense.

You should not consider buying a Bullmastiff if you live in a flat or apartment, as it will be difficult for you to give the dog the necessary exercise. Running your dog loose in the local park is not advisable unless you have complete and total control over him. Remember, the dog was bred to be a fearless protector and therefore dominant. No amount of spoiling or pampering will affect his genetic make-up.

Since the breed is relatively unknown, many people out with their dogs will not know a Bullmastiff or his temperament, often mistaking him for a Boxer cross or some form of Mastiff. Unaware of the defensive nature of the Bullmastiff, they may allow their dogs to be totally uninhibited and free. Flare-ups will occur if a dog running loose in the park challenges your Bullmastiff. Your Bullmastiff should not be criticised for being antagonistic to male dogs challenging him as this is a natural reaction. However, considering the size discrepancy, a defensive snap by the Bullmastiff could be fatal to the interloper. Bullmastiffs will normally tolerate strange female dogs as long as they are submissive. This also applies to neutered males.

For a Bullmastiff owner it is best to avoid confrontation. It is sometimes very aggravating while trying to exercise your dog to encounter so many owners who allow their dogs to run freely, exercising no control over them

from left:Stoneglad Vouge, NJW-11 Rambull's Oh Happy Day, Int.No.Se.Fin.Ch Rambull's Lily Of The Valley, Int.GB.No.Se.Fin.Ch King Of Scalebour At Garmondsway JW, Int.No.Se.Fin.Ch Rambull's New Wildwood Flower

Shayla's Brok, aged two, with puppy and baby.

whatsoever. However, this does not reduce the responsibility of the Bullmastiff owner to avoid such confrontations. Any irresponsible attitude by a Bullmastiff owner is detrimental to the owner, the dog, the breed, and the public. Although the dog is a soft, loving pet to his family, any challenge by a foolish or misguided dog or a malevolent owner will cause an aggressive response from your Bullmastiff – and you will be held responsible!

Family? What is the dog's family? It is anyone you choose in your close family relationship: friends, parents, the postman, all those you regard as familiar characters, the people with whom you feel safe and secure. Your Bullmastiff will never guard against his 'family', so consider this fact when you introduce your dog to other people. Other 'non-family' associates will be treated as outsiders.

The Bullmastiff is not a breed that approaches each new person with growls and snarls of rejection, but is a confident dog who knows his own worth. Under your guidance he will admit strangers into your home, but he will always keep an eye on them.

The key is the tone of your voice. If it is relaxed, so is his manner. If your voice is agitated or raised in anger or excitement he will be wary. In such a situation it would be very unwise for someone to move towards you quickly, even in jest, as your dog will step in to protect you.

British breed judge Mr H E Price of the Lombardy affix says that one of the first questions a prospective newcomer to the breed will ask is, 'What are they like with children?'

His answer is as follows:

Personally I firmly believe that children should not be left alone with any dog, large or small. Inevitably, accidents will happen. We have had

Can Am Ch Shayla's Keeper Alargh Ddu, the only Bullmastiff to win both the Canadian and the American National Speciality Shows. Bred by Jan Scholl and the author.

Librrani's Eleanor Gone In 60 Sec (Photo Credit: J. Baneman)

one or two such incidents in Great Britain that the press and television reporters have treated sensationally. Much of what has been said is inaccurate. In my experience, covering a great many years and a fair number of dogs, there is no safer dog than a Bullmastiff with children! For some reason hard to define they will tolerate much from a young child to which they would most certainly object from an adult, and they make excellent guard dogs for 'their' children.

Can Am Ch Shayla's Karleigh Alargh Ddu, bred by Jan Scholl and the author.

All dogs of any breed, particularly the large guarding breeds, should be taught obedience from an early age together with respect for and tolerance of children. Similarly, parents must educate their children to realise a dog is not a toy to be played with. A little common sense would prevent most accidents. If a dog is known to be aggressive, special care must be taken where children are involved. Remember: you are the controller. Watch your voice and consider your responsibility to your dog and your guests. What do you think would happen if your dog was lying quietly in the front hall and your child, who had been playing outside with a friend, suddenly burst through the front door, shrieking in excitement and hotly pursued by his pal? Think about it. These are some of the responsibilities an adult owner must consider when owning this large, impressive, powerful yet soft and gentle dog. Which part of the dog's disposition you see depends on you.

When you bring home a cute little eight-week-old pup, his soft, beseeching eyes will tug at your heartstrings. Until one year of age he will be gaining approximately 4.5kg (10lb) each month. At nine months this amounts to a large 41kg (90lb) bundle of fun who is still a puppy at heart and who still thinks he can leap on to your lap. He may be big and heavy, but he is still a baby. This exuberant and large bab You may be used to the size of your pet but those around you may not be so keen.

One thing is sure: if you do allow a Bullmastiff to be your friend, you will be converted for life and he will give you many years of loyalty, love protection, warmth and affection.

CHAPTER TWO

Origin And Development

The antiquity of the English Mastiff has been doubted by many who believe the breed as we know it today to be a relatively new one. This is true, but the same can be said of any current breed: the dog we see today is the form presently known to us. What must not be overlooked in our tunnel vision of pure-bred pedigrees is that all our accepted breeds have evolved through the centuries from some medieval or earlier ancestor. The word that confuses most people is mastiff. People suppose the word means massive, when the derivation has nothing to do with size but comes from an old English phrase 'masse thefe' meaning to master a thief – in other words, a thief-catcher. Unlike today's meaning of 'thief', a medieval thief sometimes had four legs, not just two. Dogs in medieval times were not kept for fancy; they had to earn their daily portion of food. Early dogs, by natural selection against the elements and predators, had to be big and strong. Early man harnessed the dog's natural territorial capabilities to guard flocks and herds against wolves and other dangerous predators. Pictures of dogs resembling mastiffs have been seen on the walls of Egyptian tombs 3000 years old.

The Old English Mastiff was the descendant of the Celtic war dog that fought alongside his master in 55 BC and terrified the Roman soldiers during the punitive invasion of Britain by Julius Caesar. Had it not been for the fact that the elephant the Romans had brought with them trumpeted in fear and scared the Celts, the Romans would probably have lost the day. The strength and size of these dogs so impressed them that they took some home to Rome to fight in their arenas.

The early Briton referred to his canine companion as a mastiff. His counterpart on the European continent referred to his equivalent as a dogue (dog). When Norman French was imposed on Britain after William the Conqueror succeeded at the battle of Hastings in 1066, the different references to the same animal caused misunderstanding. The European masters believed the Anglo Saxon was calling his dogue a massive (mastiff) dog.

Before William's arrival, not only did the Anglo Saxons keep dogs for personal protection, but their Anglo Saxon lords made it illegal to do otherwise. In each village the King's representative, the Regarder, made sure that for every two villeins (peasants) there was one mastiff. The reasoning behind this was that the villagers' dogs would be used to keep down the number of wild animals that might prey on the King's deer. This put the onus of deer protection on the villagers, although they were not allowed to sample the fruits of their labour.

The Regarder carried with him a mastiff gauge (see over). Through living under the protection of man for so long, smaller mastiffs that would otherwise have disappeared through natural selection had survived. If these smaller mastiffs could squeeze through the gauge, they were considered harmless as deer runners. Those mastiffs too large for the gauge had to have three toes from one of the front feet removed to prevent their running the King's deer. This was done by taking a chisel and a mallet and removing the toes, known as expeditation.

The smaller dog was the Bulldog, the larger one the Old English, or Giant, Mastiff. Many centuries passed in their development, but both types were still descended from the same common animal.

Bull-baiting was outlawed by Queen Victoria in 1835. The law was ignored for about 10 years. By the mid-19th century a big, tough, heavy, aggressive Bulldog was still being bred: a prime animal for holding a bull immobile by its top lip, but not really big enough to overpower a man.

The Giant Mastiff,on the other hand, was big and strong but did not have tenacity and aggression. The Mastiff's fighting and aggressive temperament had been lost over the years to produce a large, impressive dog that was tied in the daytime, but allowed to roam at night.

At the beginning of the 19th century parts of the feudal system were still operating in Great Britain. The aristocrats had land, wealth, big houses and estates; the common working man had very little, and usually not enough food to feed his hungry family. Men were ready to take risks to provide for their starving families by poaching game from the big estate, especially if the estate owner had an abundance of game and little use for it except as recreational hunting.

The estate owners employed gamekeepers. As the 19th century progressed poachers began to take quite a toll on the estate's game resources, and the gamekeepers were hard pressed to keep up with the increasing number of infractions. Poachers had learned that there was safety in numbers, poaching in gangs so that they hopelessly outnumbered the lone gamekeeper. It was not uncommon for gamekeepers to be found dead or badly wounded; the poachers had no intention of being caught, as the

Engraving of Duke of Hamilton with Bulldog, 1790.

penalty for poaching was death or deportation. Against odds like this poachers considered the murder of a gamekeeper in the dark of night well worth the risk.

Life was very uncertain for the gamekeepers and even more frustrating for the estate owners. They knew that local villagers, who by day touched their caps and bid them 'Good day', were the same villains who marauded in gangs at night to steal their game.

Gamekeepers had always had dogs of the terrier type to control vermin, or lurcher-type dogs to control rabbits and hares. Although well suited for this specialised work, they were most ineffective as personal guards. The gamekeepers needed a dog that was rough and tough and could take the physical abuse of kicking, punching, even blows from a club, or anything a desperate man in fear of being caught might inflict. The dog needed to be quiet and able to lie unnoticed and unseen in a thicket until ordered to take his man. To this end a brindle dog was preferred. In the early morning or late evening when most poaching was done, the brindle's stripes allowed him to blend into the background. Many gamekeepers bluffed the presence of a dog when in fact there was none, as it was well known to poachers that the dog's colour rendered him practically invisible. The fawn colour appeared as more fawn mastiffs were introduced in some areas, and red, with the secret interbreeding with the Dogue de Bordeaux. This dog resembles a coarse version of the earlier type of Bullmastiff, making it relatively easy to introduce the red colour by secret breeding, secret because the early breeders wanted their dogs to have the status of pure bred rather than cross bred animals. The first fancier to exhibit red Bullmastiffs was excused from the ring and asked to take his 'long legged red Bulldogs' with him.

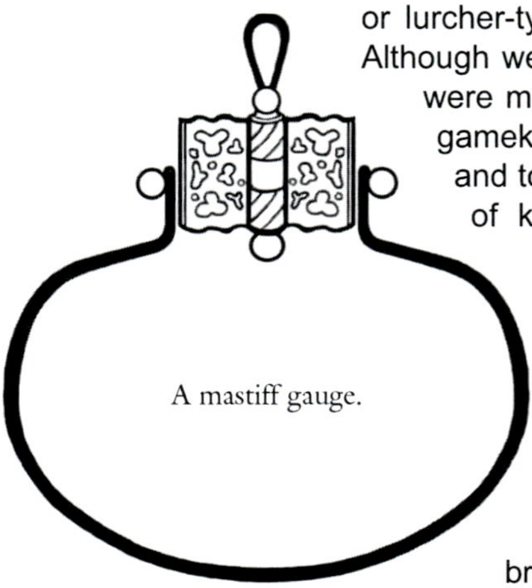

A mastiff gauge.

The dog needed to be able to communicate silently with his master to alert him if someone was moving nearby, giving the element of surprise to the gamekeeper. The Bullmastiff communicated with the gamekeeper by ear movement and wrinkling its

A typical old time Mastiff.

brow when someone was approaching, and this warning was all the gamekeeper needed.

The need for the dog to go instantly on command from a lying position to a fast, forward charge demanded well-developed thighs and hindquarters, especially in the area between the stifle and hock known as the second thigh. This muscular second thigh is the primary source of power, permitting the dog to vault forwards from a lying position to a full charge, and even swapping ends like a charging rhinocerou!.This was effected by the Gamekeeper sitting with his hand on the dog's fore head (normally relaxed, wrinkling his brow when perhaps the sound was too quiet for the Gamekeeper to hear.

Various mastiff types had been tried, but none seemed to suit the need completely. Some gamekeepers introduced European mastiffs they had seen at the popular London shows into their breeding program. In his search for the night dog he so desperately needed the gamekeeper interbred such dogs as the Great Dane, St Bernard, Dogue de Bordeaux, Dalmatian, or any other breed he felt might help him. These strange mixtures of gamekeepers' night dogs were a motley crowd. Depending on the criteria of individual gamekeepers, dogs were developed along individual lines, but none quite came up to expectations.

Results were not convincing until the appearance of the straight cross of the Bulldog and the Giant Mastiff (see diagram above), referred to in different circles as Bandog, Night Dog, Tie Dog and the Bull-and-Mastiff. This straight cross produced excellent results. The dog was a simple cross of the Bulldog of the time (a much heavier and larger version of the animal we know today, referred to in history books as the Butcher's Dog) and the Old English Giant Mastiff.

It seems ironic that the two types of medieval dogs used to protect against thieves should join up many centuries later to catch poachers. It was a common understanding among pioneer Bullmastiff breeders that by the time deliberate crosses of the two types of dogs had been made to produce the Bull and Mastiff, some shrewd gamekeepers had already recognised the natural cross of these two breeds and were using them.

Depending on the lineage and source of this new found cross, the temperament was often unpredictable. Some were too large and lethargic, others were too aggressive and injured their quarry. The gamekeeper needed a correct balance of these two breeds, large enough to knock a man down and hold him until he could be apprehended, and yet small enough to be quick, tenacious and aggressive enough to pursue a man on command with vigour and enthusiasm. The gamekeeper did not want the quarry mauled or injured; he simply wanted to turn him over to the Bailiff for imprisonment or deportation, getting him well away from his estate.

One fancier quick to recognise the usefulness of this dog for both estate guarding and police work was a man by the name of S E Moseley, of Hamil Burslem, Staffordshire. He calculated that a correct blending of 60% Mastiff and 40% Bulldog would solve the criteria needed by gamekeepers and law enforcement officers alike. He therefore took a straight cross of 50% Bulldog and 50% Mastiff (the Bull and Mastiff) and bred it with a 100% Mastiff, which resulted in a litter of puppies which were 75% Mastiff and 25% Bulldog. This

A B C

Bulldog: Ch Pugilist Farcroft Fidelity. Mastiff: Ch Crown Prince.

Forty percent from the old-type Bulldog lilke (A) and sixty percent from the Giant Mastiff like (C) went into the making of the Bullmastiff (B).

animal he bred to a 50:50 type to obtain a dog 62.5% Mastiff and 37.5% Bulldog. The closer percentage of 60:40 was adjusted by selectively breeding to other lines where genetics had produced a slightly different mix.

Local influence of type was affected by interpretation to produce bullier dogs in the north of England, more mastiff type in the south. However, in 1924, a consensus of the early breeders produced the first Kennel Club Standard, and the Bullmastiff (one word) was born.

Mr Moseley first showed one of his dogs on 6 August 1925 at Bagnall, Staffordshire, under judge R T Baines, when one class was scheduled for the breed. The dog, Farcroft Fidelity (facing page), was the first dog of the breed ever shown as a Bullmastiff. Ironically in true Bullmastiff manner Farcroft Fidelity's dam, Farcroft Faithful, died protecting her owner from poachers on the Yorkshire Moors. Her owner carried her two miles and buried her where the family could see her grave from the house.

The breed progressed until in 1928 The Kennel Club granted Challenge Certificates (CCs) for the breed at four shows: Crufts, Manchester, The Kennel Club, and Birmingham. The judge, Mr H P Brown, awarded the first CCs to the breed at the Crufts show; the dog CC to Tiger Prince, owned by Vic Smith of Pridzor Kennels, the bitch CC to Mr Moseley's Farcroft Silvo.

Farcroft Silvo went on to be the first-ever champion in the breed and during her lifetime earned herself 14 CCs. In Britain, three CCs are needed before a dog becomes a champion; Farcroft Silvo acquired her 3rd CC, and therefore her title, under judge R S Whitson. Prior to this, on 28 February 1928 at Newcastle, Farcroft Silvo was the first Bullmastiff to go Best in Show (BIS) (any variety or sex). This was truly a magnificent distinction for a dog whose breed had only recently gained recognition.

Moseley was an enthusiastic advocate of the breed and his kennel name of Farcroft was soon to be seen wherever he could introduce it. In fact it is questionable whether the Bullmastiff would have become so popular had it not been for his persistence in promoting the breed; he was convinced it would make an excellent police dog and was successful in its introduction in many areas. It is only fitting that a female from his line, Farcroft Silvo, was the first champion and BIS.

Other formative kennels who made significant contributions to the early breed were Bulmas, Oldwell, Harbex, Bulstaff, Kelwall, Mulorna, Rhodenhurst, Pridzor (see page 21), Marbette, and many, many others too numerous to list.

In the years after the recognition of the breed, hard work by the founder breeders produced an impressive guard dog, admired all over the world and imported into many countries where men no longer needed to guard their pheasants or deer, but their personal property.

Farcroft Fidelity.

Bull-and-Mastiff and the Bull/Mastiff Cross, and even the term 'Bullmastiff' that we use today was not unknown. We can therefore safely assume that this was when the first serious attempt to create our breed was made. In the early 1900s the Bullmastiff was becoming established, often being used as a guard dog.

The first world war devastated the breed, setting progress back for years. In the early 1920s Frank Moseley came on the scene. His Farcroft Bullmastiffs must be behind every modern Bullmastiff. His aim was to popularise and standardise the breed type and this was the beginning of pedigree Bullmastiffs. Thanks to his efforts The Kennel Club recognised the breed in 1924 and the breed steadily gained popularity. Several celebrities owned Bullmastiffs: HRH The Duke of Gloucester, Sir Gordon Richards and Rafael Sabatini, the famous author, among others. Vic Smith, another founder of the breed, went down in history when he took the very first Dog Challenge Certificate (CC).

The Second World War saw the end of this period of development of the Bullmastiff. Many went out of the breed, leaving just a handful of dedicated

Can Am Can BISS Banbury's Quintessential Lyric CD CGN
(Photo courtesy L. & P. Rehsler)

breeders, fortunately with a good nucleus of stock. It was then that the Bullmastiff as we know it today was created, mainly through Cyril Leeke's Bulmas and Mr Higginson's Stanfell kennels. These established the type and head style we know today, very different from the long-muzzled, snipey pre-war dogs.

We have developed a Bullmastiff far different from that of our ancestors. Today our best have good square skulls. Muzzles are short, perhaps too short for my liking; I prefer them one third of the overall head length. Mouths are particularly good, with perfect or near-perfect level bites, the broad underjaw with teeth in a straight line giving a square-cut appearance to the muzzle. Though it is often said heads are not everything it is a hard fact that without a good head the Bullmastiff is nothing!

THE BRINDLE BULLMASTIFF

It is probably entirely due to Mr and Mrs Warren (not to be confused with our present-day Gerald Warren) of the Harbex kennel that brindles did not become extinct during the second world war. They alone managed to bring this colour through these difficult years, and to them must go all of the credit for providing the base on which to build this colour. If they had not done so the colour would have had to be reintroduced from another breed. Certainly, in the early post-war years Ted and Florrie Warren were the only ones interested in breeding this colour. In view of the popularity of the brindle today I find this strange. Their most notable brindles were Grim and Chips of Harbex and it is a fact that every brindle in Great Britain today is descended from Harbex stock.

Canadian Champion Brutus of Ellisdene
(Photo curtesy of B. & J. Walkey)

The brindle remained almost unnoticed until in the early 1960s two entirely separate kennels took up the colour almost simultaneously. The late Mrs L Parkes of the Silverfarm affix bought a brindle dog, Sealskin of Harbex, not a very good specimen of the breed. Walter and Lyn Pratt of Kelwall took one of their red bitches to a Harbex dog to be mated, and this was the foundation of both kennels of brindle Bullmastiffs. Both soon made probably the greatest step forward for this colour: Walter and Lyn produced a good red brindle bitch and Mrs Parkes bred the famous Copper of Silverfarm. Both were shown fearlessly, yet neither got the success they deserved, as many judges were reluctant even to consider a brindle. Mrs Parkes continued to breed and exhibit the colour against all odds, often standing unnoticed in the class. She was a lady of great determination; a lesser person would have given up the struggle. It is perhaps of interest that her breeding policy was to mate her brindle bitches to Mrs D M Price's red dogs to keep the correct colour (dark or black markings on a red or orange background). By now the brindle was gaining in popularity and several prominent kennels were interested. Harry Collias (Oldwell) bred and exhibited several very good dogs, while Ralph and Ruth Short (Bulstaff), Douglas Oliff and Granville Blount (Naukeen) were also active. Mrs D M Price (Lombardy) had some success following a mating to Ch Clyde. Probably one of the most prominent brindle enthusiasts is Jim Leeson (Pitman's). His Ch Pitman's Deputy, a most prolific sire, will be found in many pedigrees. Pitman's Smart Alex, another prominent sire and in my personal opinion the best brindle ever, Pitman's Ambassador and Ch Pitman's Dark Prince have sired many of today's brindles.It is fair to say that the brindle today is the equal of any self colour, in many cases the superior. It has had a difficult time, but the hard work put in by these dedicated people has now paid off It is a fact

Am Ch. Blackslate's Improper Bostonian (Photo curtesy of V. Rowland)

that every brindle in Great Britain today is descended from Harbex stock. The brindle remained almost unnoticed until in the early 1960s two entirely separate kennels took up the colour almost simultaneously. The late Mrs L Parkes of the Silverfarm affix bought a brindle dog, Sealskin of Harbex, not a very good specimen of the breed. Walter and Lyn Pratt of Kelwall took one of their red bitches to a Harbex dog to be mated, and this was the foundation of both kennels of brindle Bullmastiffs. Both soon made probably the greatest step forward for this colour: Walter and Lyn produced a good red brindle bitch and Mrs Parkes bred the famous Copper of Silverfarm. Both were shown fearlessly, yet neither got the success they deserved, as many judges were reluctant even to consider a brindle.

Mrs Parkes continued to breed and exhibit the colour against all odds, often standing unnoticed in the class. She was a lady of great determination; a lesser person would have given up the struggle.

CHAPTER THREE

Choosing a Puppy

What Makes a Puppy Special?

In the garden: Heroguardian Lady Ana Solo (Sadie) aged 19 months, with Anna Perry aged 13 months.

Why is every puppy so cute? Like everything else in life, beauty is in the eye of the beholder. What most people do not realise is that their concept of beauty has evolved as a result of incidents that have occurred throughout their lives. Was it the way your parents did certain things? Was it a memory left behind after some pleasant occasion in your life? Whatever it was, each person has individual tastes and it is the gratification of these that brings happiness.

The reasons are just the same when it comes to a Bullmastiff puppy. Ask yourself why you'd like a Bullmastiff. What made you first decide to take a puppy home to be part of your life? The chances are somewhere, sometime you saw a Bullmastiff that just stole your heart and now you want to fill that memory by taking one home to be a part of your life.

Visiting the Breeder

What do you look for when you visit a breeder to choose your puppy? To the layman most puppies look the same no matter what breed, so make sure that you do not make a hurried choice and take the wrong puppy home.

If you want a nice, loving, good old-fashioned pet to take for walks, someone to keep you company at night, someone to love, with never a thought of showing or breeding, you do not need to read any further. Let your heart decide, go to the end of this chapter and start reading again at Ready to Go.

Banbury's Who's Your Daddy?

If you are looking for a show dog, your choice will have to be more selective. Most breeders will let you see the litter at about eight weeks of age, a very special age to which most people do not really give enough importance.

Between the time of birth and four weeks of age, puppies investigate anything new. This is nature's way of making sure that newborns familiarise themselves with their territory for security's sake. When danger threatens, the pups will run to the mother or the den for safety, ensuring survival.

Between the age of four and eight weeks, the puppies will reverse this attitude. Instead of running to everything new, they run away and reject anything different. This is another of nature's survival tactics. In the wild the mother usually takes her pups out of the den after four weeks and introduces them to the world. At this stage pups stay close to her, or to the den when she leaves to go hunting. At the sign of anything new and strange, instead of running to investigate as they would have done a week before, the pups run to the things they know to be safe: the den and the mother. This ensures survival, preventing them from being eaten as a result of running towards a predator.

What does this mean to you as a prospective puppy owner? In the first weeks of adoption, your puppy will be very anxious and nervous of new situations. As a new owner you must be patient and reassure the little dog if he baulks or reacts to anything new in a scared or nervous fashion. If you do this you will replace the mother in the puppy's mind and develop a bond between you and the little dog, ensuring a well-adjusted pet that will not jump or over-react at the slightest thing.

When you go to see the breeder and the new litter, ask the breeder to let you see the parents. If both are not available there will usually be a photo of the father at least, and the mother will be there with the puppies. Remember that the puppy will grow up to resemble one or both of the

Opalguard pups at six weeks

parents to some extent, so take a careful look at the mother and father. If you do not particularly like what you see, leave immediately. If you stay, the puppy will win your heart anyway and you will end up with a dog whose appearance you do not like. According to the Bullmastiff standard, all Bullmastiffs should look the same, but this is never true in life no matter what you consider. There will be minor differences in looks, colour and type. So if you do not like the parents, go home. There will always be another day for you to choose a puppy. You will have the love of this dog for many years, so do not choose in haste and repent at leisure.

So you have decided you like the look of the parents, that is why you are still here. Good. Now we must get down to the serious business of how to choose. Bear in mind that each line of dogs has a particular growth pattern, and only the breeder can tell you what it is; all the following advice will be modified by this fact. However, it will give you some pointers as to which questions to ask, and certain things are true no matter what the growth patterns are.

Puppy Parts

We will start by taking the individual parts of the dog, and go over them one by one.

The Head

Even at the tender age of a few weeks, the head (cranium) of the Bullmastiff will be in evidence as a cube: whichever way you look at the head it will be square. This viewing does not include the muzzle, jaw or ears; just the head itself. You should be able to see a square head easily.

Looking at the head from the top or the front, the eyes should be at the front corners of the head. Eyes closer together indicate a narrow head or incorrect positioning of the eyes which will give an unnatural appearance. The attachment of the ears should be in line with the positioning of the eyes, so that the eyes are at the 'front' corners, and the ear attachment at the 'back' corners. This will ensure you have a dog with a wide-set, square-looking head. At this time in the puppy's life the ears will look exceptionally big and may hang down to the bottom of its jaw. The only guide to the adult animal is the parents.

The Muzzle

The vertical attachment of the muzzle should be below the eyes and the width of the muzzle at this age should appear almost as wide at the front as it does at the point of attachment. In profile, the puppy may appear to have a large lump on the bridge of its nose. This is perfectly normal. This 'extra' nose will be displaced in the next few weeks as the puppy's muzzle grows. When you check the teeth, the bite should be level, or slightly overshot. Overshot? Yes! The puppy's muzzle is made up of the upper mandible, which is attached to the skull, and the lower jaw, which grows

Bullmastiff bitch cleaning her sleepy puppy. Pup's eyes are not yet open.

Early socialisation.

independently from the mandible. The two parts see-saw as the puppy grows, so if the bite is as described the chances are your puppy will end up with a correct bite. If the teeth are undershot at this age, you stand a good chance of the mature dog having a bad underbite. The extent to which this occurs will depend on the line and you must ask your breeder about this. Inside the mouth, the incisor teeth should be even and the canines well spaced. The canines give the dog the wide, square muzzle so a puppy with narrow canines will result in a snipey-nosed dog.

The Neck

The roly-poly puppy you see before you will one day be a big dog. Proportions will change as in every living animal. However, if you look at the parents and like the type of neck each has, and they are similar, the chances are the puppy's neck will be about the same. A puppy's neck is short anyway, but look carefully. If his head seems to be sitting in the shoulders, he may have little or no neck and even a puppy should be able to show a certain amount of neck at this age. If his head movement seems a little stilted, look elsewhere in the litter. Conversely, giraffe necks are equally as undesirable.

The Body

Although only a diminutive of his parents, the squareness or otherwise of the body will be very evident. Stand the puppy up on a level surface and you should see easily whether the dog looks long in the body or short in the leg. When viewed from the side, the distance from the fore chest to the back of the thighs should roughly equal the height of the dog at the top of the shoulders (withers) even at this age. You will also be able to see if the puppy has sufficient brisket which should reach at least to his elbows. Take a look at the distance from the point of his elbow to the ground. Is it about half the height of the dog from the shoulder to the ground? Is his hock about one third of the height of the dog at the shoulder? Look at him from the front to make sure he is nice and broad in the chest; you do not

Four weeks old (bred by the author).

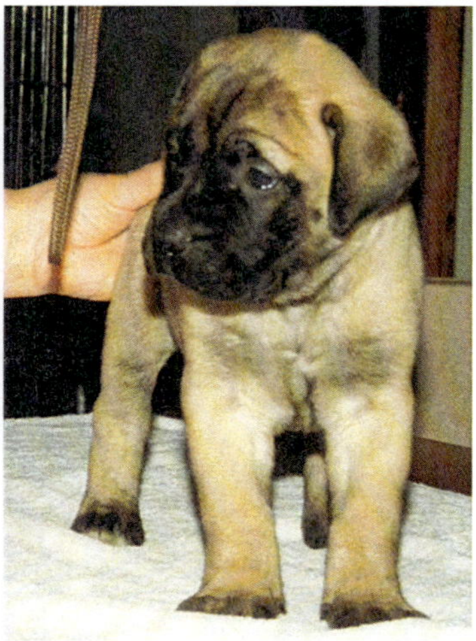

Five weeks old.

Seven weeks old.

Eight weeks old.

want a narrow chested dog! His rear end should be almost as broad as his front. If it is considerably narrower than his front, you are witnessing Bulldog genes at work and your dog will grow up to be 'bully'.

Although these glimpses will be brief, and with full knowledge that he has a whole lifetime of growing ahead of him, such obvious glaring faults will be seen if they are extreme. Although it may fall within the widest interpretation of the standard, if the puppy is extreme in any area now the chances of changing dramatically are slight.

The Tail

Many people look at puppies and try to guess their eventual size by the enormity of its paws. You are looking at the wrong place, however; all that you will be able to tell is that a Bullmastiff has enormous feet compared to a Border Terrier puppy! Allowing for the absence of crank or stunted versions, take a look at his tail. In the mature Bullmastiff, the best kind of tail should reach the hock. What about the puppy you are considering? Go on, take it and see where it reaches. A puppy whose tail reaches to or past his hock is probably a big dog in the making. The reverse also applies.

A LAST CHECK

Before you snatch the puppy up and run home, a few more tips. Put him on the floor and watch him run around. The movement should be easy, balanced, and not narrow or single tracking. No glaring structural faults like cow hocks. This would show faulty skeletal structure.

What about his colour? In most cases, Bullmastiffs do not turn out to be the colour you expect when they are puppies. At birth most puppies are very dark, sometimes appearing black. The darker the puppy at birth the richer and deeper the colour at maturity. The dark colouring gradually goes until at about one year the colour is true and clear. The last vestiges of this darkness are usually a line down the back and the tip of the tail. So this is quite normal, unless the parents are still covered with a sooty shading, called pencilling, in areas such as the chest, neck and face. The standard is very specific that the colour has to be clear. If your puppy's parents are like this, your puppy will probably be the same. This sootiness is produced by too close a breeding, or by failing to adhere to the correct colour breeding patterns as first described by Eric Makins and Arthur Craven, two Bullmastiff pioneers from the early part of this century. This comment refers to fawns and reds, not brindles.

The standard permits a small amount of white on the chest. The white is referred to as permissible but undesirable, except for a small white patch. The operative word here is small: it does not mean white blazes reaching from the chin to the navel. Such dogs still appear in the show ring and, while judges endorse their presence with awards, such deviations will perpetuate. The presence of any white indicates the presence of Bulldog genes, of which the Bullmastiff carries 40%. If your puppy shows more white than an area about the size of a 50 pence piece, talk to the breeder. Some lines that show a little white at a few weeks lose it as the chest of the dog develops and in some cases seems to 'fold inwards'. Although this does not alter the genetic involvement, visually it reduces and sometimes disappears altogether.

Ready To Go

So you have gone through all the above and you have not left yet. Well, I suppose all that matters now is to pick the right one and be on your way. Right? Wrong! Talk to the breeder about the type of dog you would like to fit in with your family structure. Do you want a quiet dog, a barker, a dominant one, or a quiet pet to take with you wherever you go? The only person who can point out these things is the breeder. He knows his dogs, his line, his puppies' dispositions and whom they will suit best. Discuss these points truthfully and candidly because the one thing that you, the breeder, and the puppy do not want is your returning in a few days time, puppy under your arm, with a distressed look on all your faces telling everyone that you are not compatible. Be sensible: talk to the breeder. If you are the tiniest bit hesitant, go home and come back tomorrow. The breeder will understand and appreciate your action. One thing for which you must strive is that you, the breeder and the puppy are totally happy about the step you are about to make.

If you can answer 'yes' to all the questions asked in the above section you will soon be the owner of a Bullmastiff puppy.

A reputable breeder will advise you when the pup was wormed, the correct worming programme to follow and when he is due for his first vaccination. In the United Kingdom, the puppy is unlikely to have been vaccinated whilst still with the breeder unless you are purchasing an older puppy; in this case be sure to collect the vaccination card with the puppy.

Courtenay's Pride Puppy

One more thing before you go. Talk to the breeder about his feeding programme. He has raised the parent dogs you liked so much and a fine litter of puppies. This did not happen by accident; it was by careful planning, knowledge and expertise. Your breeder will be only too pleased to provide you with a puppy pack which will contain all the information you need to know in the first important year of your puppy's life. If at any time you need further advice or help, do not ask the man next door; ask your breeder, who will willingly help you. **Congratulations! You are now the proud owner of a fine Bullmastiff puppy.**

CHAPTER FOUR

Maintenance and Grooming

Did you ever wonder why some Bullmastiffs look stunning even to a bystander while others look quite ordinary?

Just as a clean, shiny car looks appealing compared to a dirty, unkempt one so it is with everything in life – including a Bullmastiff. The original Bullmastiffs were hard-working country dogs who spent most of their lives outside in the rain and inclement weather. Their one aim in life was to catch poachers, though later in the evening they thoroughly appreciated a warm place by the fire after a good supper. The gamekeepers kept their dogs healthy and strong but aesthetics were the last thing on their minds. As society changed, so more attention was given to the Bullmastiff's appearance as well as the work he did.

The Bullmastiff's weatherproof coat takes care of his insulation and waterproofing from the elements. However, modern-day owners expect their dogs to be compatible with their living conditions and to blend into the family structure without offence to the eye or nose, so some grooming is necessary. As has already been indicated, the Bullmastiff's coat type requires minimum work to keep it in good condition. However, there are a number of small maintenance items that will make your Bullmastiff look twice the dog.

The Head

Ears

The Bullmastiff's ears are drop ears and so hang down naturally. Their closeness to the side of the head can sometimes close off the opening of the ear canal, restricting air circulation, and the natural body heat causes the ear canals to overheat. This results in the ear canal filling up with a smelly, waxy substance that is very unpleasant and must be removed. Use a piece of cotton wool or a commercial cotton swab, but be sure to clean

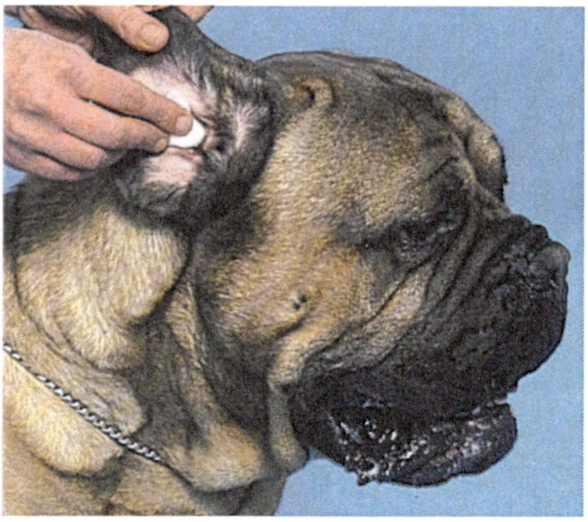

Cleaning the ears.

Nylabone products help to prevent tartar – and are fun to chew as well.

only the inside of the ear where you can see. Do not poke down into the ear canal, as any unqualified probing or a sudden movement by the dog can lead to a perforated ear drum. A mixture of mild soap and water or any patent ear cleaner will clean off this waxy substance. At the same time, look at the colour of the inside of the leather to see if it looks reddened or sore. If so, the chances are that the dog is carrying an infection. Do not attempt to remedy this yourself but contact your veterinary surgeon.

If a dark, smelly substance similar to wax still persists after the ears have been cleaned the dog may be carrying mites in the lower part of the ear canal. Once again, do not attempt to remedy this yourself. This is a job for a qualified vet, not an amateur.

Eyes

The Bullmastiff does not have a haw eye like the Mastiff or St Bernard. Rather, he has a nice tight eye that usually remains trouble-free. This eye may need wiping from time to time to remove any air-borne detritus or 'sleep', but generally a Bullmastiff's eyes need little or no maintenance. Should you need to clean the eyes at any time, use a solution of boric acid. Commercial preparations are readily available at most pet stores. The Bullmastiff's eyes are clear and alert. If you notice ulceration or redness, it is possible he may have caught his eye on a stick or some sharp object. However, this may also be caused by entropion (see chapter 6). Whatever you feel the problem is, contact your vet.

Mouth

The Bullmastiff has a big, strong set of teeth. These should be kept clean at all times of tartar to reduce the chance of gum diseases and future loss of teeth at a young age. A good way of cleaning your dog's teeth and keeping his gums healthy is to give him an ample supply of hard dog biscuits to crunch on. It is a good idea to teach your puppy that frequent mouth inspections are a normal, every day procedure. This will permit checks for tartar which can be removed easily in the early stages with the edge of a sharp fingernail or a tooth scaler. I do not recommend that you give bones to your Bullmastiff, as his jaws are so strong that he is likely to gnaw fragments off the bone which will lodge in his stomach, causing problems.

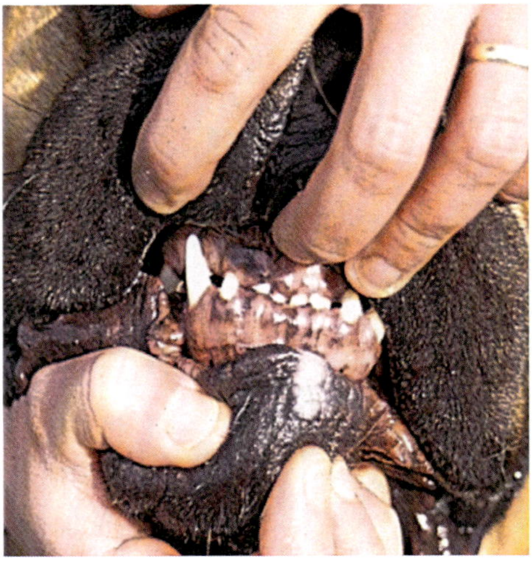

Inspect your dog's mouth and teeth regularly.

Your local pet store will also supply a range of pet toys and chews that are specially formulated to clean the teeth whilst at the same time providing enjoyment for the dog. Nylabone produce a range of strong, durable chews that enhance the dog's dental care.

Whiskers

Whiskers may be removed if the owner prefers it, but any advantage is purely aesthetic. In some cultures the dog is seen always with all normal whiskers. If you wish to remove them for show or personal preference, certain safeguards have to be followed.

Although totally unlike human shaving, the initial sensation of removing whiskers will be strange to your dog. The safest way to remove them is to insert the fingers of one hand under the lips of the dog's mouth and cut the whiskers off with scissors held in the other hand. Make sure the tips of the scissors point away from the dog's eyes in case he suddenly moves or objects to the procedure. Scissors with large, rounded tips can be purchased specifically for this task if the owner is a little nervous of having scissors around the dog's eyes. Some Bullmastiffs will allow their faces to be clipped with an electric

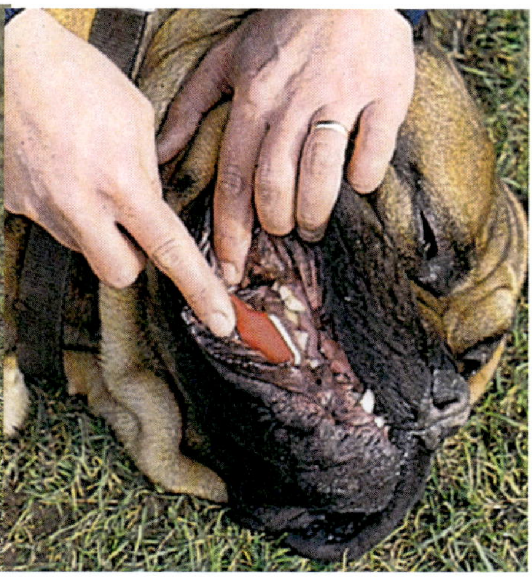

Keeping the teeth free of tartar.
Left: a Nylabone Plaque Attacker Dental Floss.
Right: using a doggy toothbrush and toothpaste.

clipper, but this takes co-operation, time, and a trusting dog.

Feet

A Bullmastiff's feet should be strong, cat-like and well knuckled. This will not come about if he spends all his time lying or standing on a carpet in front of the fire, nor if he spends most of the time on concrete: this will splay his feet. The best medium for producing good feet is rounded, coarse gravel, about the size of pea gravel. This will make the muscles of his feet work hard, strengthening and developing them. If a dog run of this kind cannot be constructed, regular, brisk walks along gravel paths will produce the same results. Running in the wet sand on a beach will also be beneficial to the feet, as long as the salt is washed off after the run to avoid irritation or rashes.

Nails

The Bullmastiff is a large and heavy dog. To balance his frame he needs to stand upright with his muscles in perfect tone. He cannot do this if his nails are so long that he has to lean back on his pasterns. Continued posture like this will develop incorrect musculature in his pasterns and the balance of the whole dog will be affected. Sensible breeders will cut the nails short at a very early age to prevent the nerve, or quick as it is sometimes called, from growing too long. If this has been done it will be easy to cut the nails ever after without any worry of cutting them too short or causing them to bleed. The dog has no natural need to dig down burrows or underground so long nails are not necessary. When he is older, your Bullmastiff will thank you for looking after his feet.

Capping

Your Bullmastiff may not object to lying on hard surfaces (Bullmastiffs rarely do) but lying down heavily will eventually wear and tear the skin around his elbows and hocks. The skin gets knocked off and calloused and a hard cap of cartilage forms to protect the area. Hair grows very slowly on a Bullmastiff at the best of times, but once this happens, no more hair! The provision of a blanket or soft bedding will reduce or eliminate conditions that cause capping.

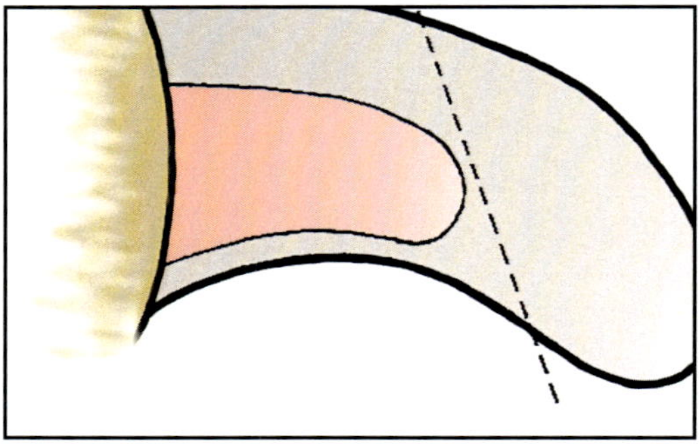

Trimming the nails. Illustration shows the position of the quick; be careful not to cut too close to it.

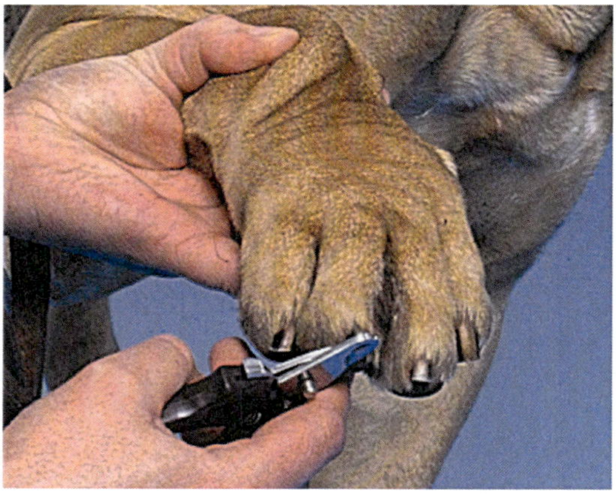

Spring loaded nail clippers are most effective on the strong nails of a Bullmastiff.

The Coat

The coat is waterproof and therefore usually looks good with very little attention. However, certain allowances have to be made if the dog lives outdoors in a dry, hot climate where the sebaceous glands of the skin have trouble keeping the coat oiled and shiny. Hot weather will also dry the skin and add to the problem. To keep the skin supple and well oiled, a rubber hound glove should be used regularly with pressure all over the body to stimulate the flow of oil and massage the skin to a supple, healthy condition.

If the undercoat is causing the coat to be dull and harsh to the touch, it is time to remove it. A wire slicker brush will do a very fine job of this and the brush can be cleaned of its dead hair with a metal comb.

If your dog has been wormed recently he will shed the dead hair in his coat. This apparently short-haired dog will seem to produce an enormous amount of loose coat.

Something else that will cause a certain amount of confusion to your dog's coat is electric light. In the autumn the colder weather causes nature to prepare your dog for winter by increasing the quantity of his coat. This change is initiated by the reducing amount of daylight hours. If your Bullmastiff spends more and more time in your house as the weather cools off, the electric light will contradict his hormones' interpretation of the shortening days. The extra light on his coat will convince the hormones that the days are getting longer again and spring will seem to be arriving early. Conversely, the increasing light and temperatures of spring will cause him to shed his undercoat as his body temperature becomes too warm. The result is the shedding of the coat in readiness for warmer days of spring whether the time is real or not. This produces dog hair everywhere, a very frustrating experience for the house-proud owner. You have two alternatives: arrange warm, comfortable accommodation outside and leave nature to her own ways, or be prepared to use a slicker brush and comb daily to relieve your Bullmastiff of his excess coat and keep your furniture and clothing hair-free.

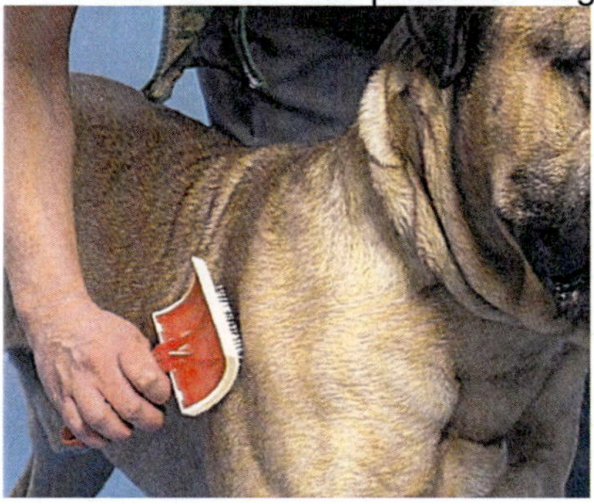

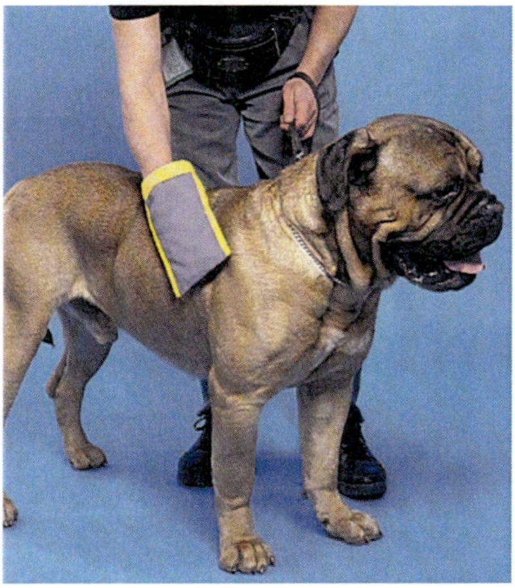

Using the slicker brush (top) and hound glove (below).

In many cases the remedy for a dirty coat is a good walk in the rain, or a drenching with a hose. Too many hot washes with shampoo will remove the oils necessary for a healthy coat, so hand washing should be done with utmost discretion.

Exposed extremities such as nose, lips, ears or even the spaces between the toes will benefit from an application of petroleum jelly or Vaseline. Your dog will appreciate such assistance to prevent cracking in hot climates. Remember not to do this to the pads; they act as a heat exchanger, so an application to this area will reduce heat loss and cause distress. If you do not believe it, watch for the damp footprints on your kitchen floor on a hot day.

Preparing for a Show

The Bullmastiff is a minimum maintenance dog. Besides the general grooming procedures described here, his natural appearance needs very little enhancing to get him ready for a show.

Depending on the cleanliness and coat condition, many Bullmastiffs go from the kennel to the show without the need for a bath. It will be necessary to clean your dog's coat if it has become soiled. Keep in mind that this working dog should have a waterproof coat; you do not want to turn up in the show ring with a Bullmastiff so recently bathed that his coat feels soft and fluffy.

You will need a few trial washes but usually, if you bathe your dog three to five days before a show, his natural oils will have returned. The required coat condition can be assisted by vigorous grooming with a rubber hound glove.

The only trimming prior to a show is the cowlicks down the back of the hind legs. These can sometimes become a little ragged and should be trimmed discreetly to enhance the line of the legs.

The flews of the Bullmastiff breed turn up at the back of the mouth, minimising any saliva or water loss in drooling or slobbering. Thankfully this removes the necessity for bibs, as seen on St Bernards, to protect the finished look while waiting to go into the ring. Some exhibitors carry a small cloth to wipe away any drooling caused through nerves, apprehension, or baiting.

Exercise

Your Bullmastiff is like a muscular athlete. When he first wakes up in the morning, some of his muscles may be stiff and tight. It is important to let your dog relax these muscles before starting exercise.

Even then, a Bullmastiff is not the kind of breed that wants to go on a five-mile jog. Exercise is necessary and important but it is amazing how little he needs to keep himself fit and healthy. Do not over-exercise your Bullmastiff, especially in the formative first year. If you take into account the weight your dog gains in that year it is easy to see that large amounts of cartilage are being formed at a very fast rate. If you over-exercise your dog, you will do a very good job of ruining his cartilaginous fibre and producing permanent damage to his skeletal structure.

A young Bullmastiff should be watched very closely. Once he has had enough exercise, let him rest. The exercise he has should be of his own making and not forced upon him by an over-enthusiastic owner who feels all big dogs need vigorous action. If you do this you will have an unhappy, and possibly permanently damaged, dog. At the age when everything is growing so fast it is easy for a young dog to over-rotate his hocks or any other joint, so treat him carefully. You should not think of him as a weakling, but as an adolescent in his formative years who needs guidance and wisdom. Depending on the growth pattern of your dog, half a mile a day may be all he wants to tackle. Some do more. The secret is to watch him. If he continuously sits down and is reluctant to follow, the chances are that he is tired and has had enough.

When he is about one year old formal exercise can begin. This should start off as good walks that do not tire him too much. Remember, it is the same distance there as back. Bullmastiffs do not mature physically until they are about three years old, so a little patience and understanding is required while this gentle giant is growing up. When he is able he will give you all the service you need and, provided you do not push him past his limits, he will reward your care with many years of faithful response.

The Older Bullmastiff

Depending on his lineage and the care he receives in the early part of his life, a Bullmastiff may start to become 'old' as early as six years of age. Each dog must be evaluated on its merits, but there are certain criteria to watch.

One of the earliest indications of pending old age is excessive amounts of stiffness and joint immobility. Arthritis can arrive very early in a Bullmastiff's life, and once arrived is there to stay. The tremendous weight on joints eventually takes its toll and, as the dog's regenerative mechanism slows down with his aging metabolism, the slide becomes one way. Luckily today's medications can relieve much of the distress as the dog moves further into his years, but always remember you will be treating a symptom and not the cause.

When this time arrives for your dog, a positive aid to his situation is to ensure that he has a warm, dry place to sleep. A little padding on his sleeping area will help his sore joints, and you should make doubly sure that his sleeping quarters are draught-free. Keep trips outdoors in wet or cold weather to a minimum and be extra patient when he is trying to manoeuvre his large frame; it may be a very painful experience for him. Stairs and narrow halls may also be monumental challenges for him to overcome, so keep this thought in mind when considering quarters for your geriatric Bullmastiff.

The arthritis may also coincide with incontinence. At first this may only show as a mild odour on the bedding, but ultimately you must address the whole problem. Medications can help here, too.

The only other common problem as the dog advances in age is failing eyesight. This is often missed because he may hide this debility for some time by using his nose and knowledge of the house. When the problem is diagnosed, a kindness to your dog would be to leave items of furniture where they have always been, and return chairs to their usual places after use.

These are all symptoms of old age, and one or more of them will occur eventually. It is at that time in the dog's life that his owner has to think carefully about the future of the relationship with his canine friend. For those not used to coping with this, read Eventide in chapter 9.

CHAPTER FIVE
Housing

Inside or Out?

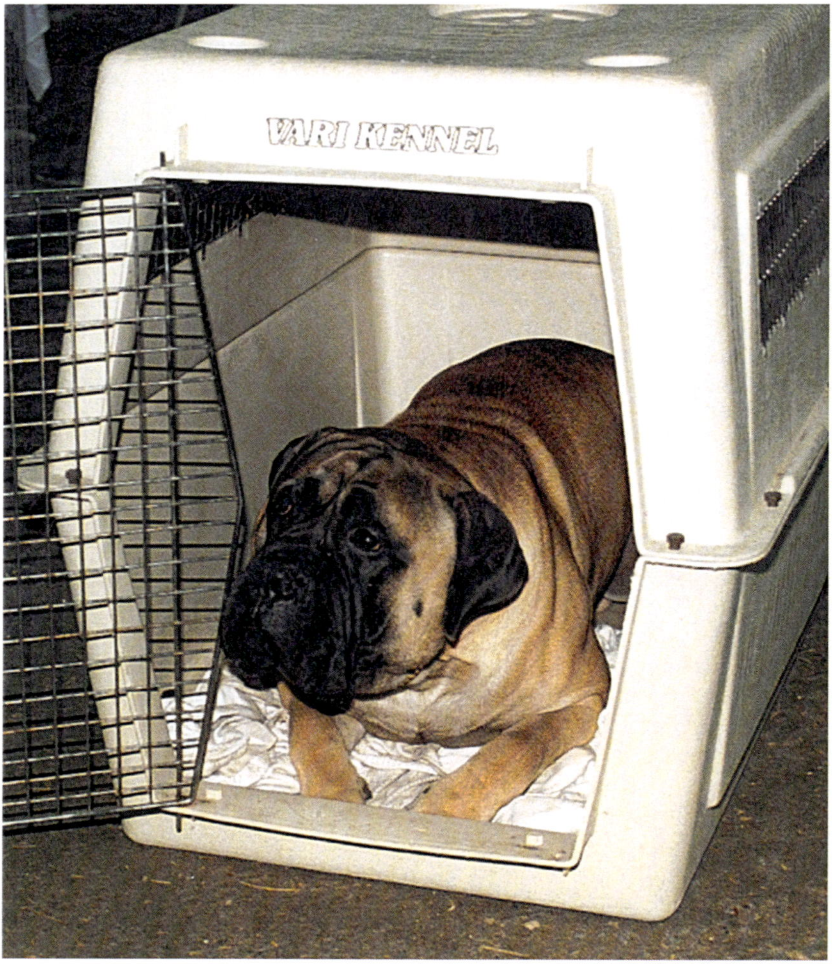

Crate for use as a doggy den in the house or car.

A major decision to be made by the senior members of the family is where your puppy is to sleep. At maturity a Bullmastiff does not take up as much room as you might first think, but it still presents a sizable space problem that must be considered ahead of time. When your new puppy arrives there will be many requests at night to take this little charmer to share one of the children's beds (or Mum and Dad's). Whoever is cited as the culprit, sooner or later a more definite decision has to be made as to where the new Bullmastiff puppy will sleep permanently. It is important for you to decide where this is to be early in the dog's life to avoid confusing him. Your Bullmastiff will want a place he can consider secure against cats and exuberant children, or just a place where he can sit quietly when life gets a little hectic.

Life will be strange to the new canine member of your family no matter what care is taken by the thoughtful owner. It is a good idea to settle the puppy into his routine as soon as possible. Like a young child, the little newcomer will quickly learn if one member of the family is willing to allow oversights when the other is not. For this reason, once you have decided whether to have inside or outside quarters, and assigned the sleeping quarters, you should keep to it regardless of the cries of woe and appeal that will arise in the first few nights from both puppy and humans. Develop your plan of strategy and remain firm. Your pup will then quickly realise there is no compromising and will settle down to the routine; house-training will soon be over and then you will have a nice, clean, happy puppy who is welcomed by everyone.

Inside

If you decide to keep the puppy inside the first challenge is house-training. When the puppy is put to bed after a riotous day of fun and play everyone is tired and of the same mind: sleep, no need to go outside. However, next morning when someone has to clean up after the little one, who will have been up longer than you, the mess and unpleasantness will be shared by all.

Puppies have an in-built aversion to soiling their own sleeping area. A good way to house train your puppy is to crate him at night, and choose a crate that is confining rather than a large one. The little puppy will hang on as long as he can as he does not want to lie in his mess. For your part, as soon as you are up in the morning, hurry him outside to your choice of toilet areas before he explodes. Bullmastiffs of all ages seem to produce a tremendous amount of waste matter: they must be hollow. This is your time to praise him generously, telling him what a good puppy he is, and do it with lots of gusto. It is much better than the alternative! Be prepared to take your puppy outside first thing in the morning, straight after each meal, and last thing at night. This amounts to at least six times each day. Up to the age of four months your puppy has very little muscle control over his inner organs so he needs to go outside every couple of hours and after each nap.

When your puppy has mastered this kindly act the next step is to allow him more liberty in his new indoor housing to see if he can be trusted until he goes outside. An enclosed area in the kitchen or utility room with a linoleum or tile floor is very forgiving in the case of accidents, and easy to clean up. Remember, control what you can. If he is good, expand the area and the trust; if he regresses, close back up. If you have to leave the house for a while, a large crate allows him freedom of movement but ensures no surprises await you on your return.

All this practice is a dry run for when he lives in the house all the time. When you are satisfied with the pup's house-training he will need a large basket or, as most people prefer, a large crate of his own. The large crate approach allows him his own in-house secure area and at awkward times, such as tradesmen coming and going, you can lock the door of the crate so you can be quite sure where he is. Crating him up saves the tradesmen a lot of worry!

The bedding area should be big enough to allow the Bullmastiff to stretch out, not just for luxury but for his health. A mature dog is likened to a muscular weight lifter. After spending many hours sleeping or resting the muscles sometimes become a little stiff or uncomfortable and it is necessary for your dog to stand, stretch and get the cramps out of them. Failure to do this will give your dog much discomfort. The breed is quite insensitive to pain especially when asleep so make sure his sleeping area has no sharp edges.

That a Bullmastiff is a large, heavy, muscled dog should be evident by now and, when he lies down, it is sometimes a great physical effort to do so quietly and gently. In many cases the dog will just drop down. After all, the shortest distance between two points is a straight line, and the Bullmastiff knows his physics! To save his joints, muscles, and general frame it is a good idea to provide him with enough padding in his bed to give him a little cushioning when he first lies down and while he sleeps. He will

The picture shows a raised sleeping area to prevent draughts. In the background is a slide which can be lifted to allow the dog access to the outside run.

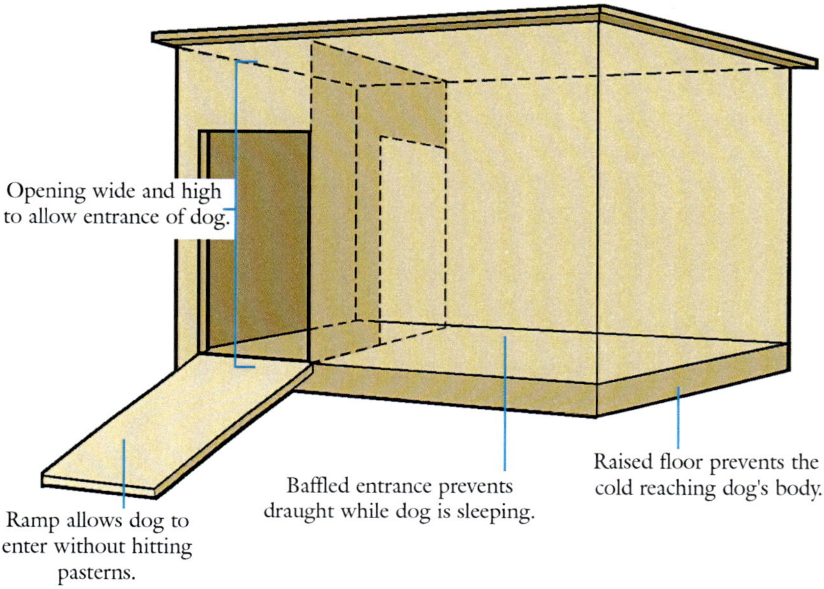

Plan of outside sleeping quarters for a Bullmastiff.

thank you in the morning. Your extra thought in providing such bedding also saves the capping of his joints described in chapter 4. When you do give him bedding be sure you treat it regularly for fleas, as such a soft, warm area is prime flea country.

Bullmastiffs need a considerable amount of water so, before he arrives at your house, decide whether to leave a dish of water with him all night or just through the day. The answer to this usually depends on your house-training successes, or lack of them.

You also need to consider how to position his bed. Strong as he is, he must not be housed where it is damp or draughty, or in a main thoroughfare. Put him in an out-of-the-way place, perhaps in a quiet corner or a dry, well-aired portion of your utility room; preferably away from the madding crowd, but in a spot from which he can investigate unknowns quickly without taking the laundry basket with him as he jumps up to see what the noise is about. He will always want to see what is going on but does not need to be in the main thoroughfare. You will appreciate a carefully chosen position when you are trying to cook supper or get the kids off to school, so think about all the options.

The bedding should be changed regularly to keep the doggy smell out of every household item and to check the flea situation. At certain times your Bullmastiff loses a lot of hair (see chapter 4). Regular bed changes ensure that dog hair is not mixed with every other household article in the near vicinity.

Outside

The Bullmastiff is well prepared for an outside life with his weatherproof coat, specially evolved for inclement weather. The original Bullmastiffs were used to living outside on their masters' estates, but modern day living puts more restrictions on the average owner than on the old-time gamekeepers. When a modern Bullmastiff is kept outside, consideration must be given not just to those factors considered in the Indoor section, but to every aspect of his life on his master's 'estate'.

The 'estate' must be clearly defined for the Bullmastiff. The safest way is to ensure that the exercise area and the whole back garden is fenced. In many cases the fence is not only to keep the dog in, establishing the limits of his territory, but to keep out casual guests such as children, meter readers, dustmen, postmen, unwanted dogs, and anyone else who should know better than to come into your back garden uninvited. The only safe way to do this is to enclose the garden with a fence at least 1.5m (5ft) in height, higher if possible. Bullmastiffs are not jumpers, but their weight can cause considerable damage. To offset this, a rail at about 1.5m high for the dog to jump against will prevent an unstrengthened fence from collapsing under the concentrated weight in one small area.

Wooden fencing is most suitable but, where this is not economically feasible, chain link is fine as long as the top is protected with a strengthened strand. Remember to make the 1.5m high rail, and do make the fence strong. It is amazing what a few jumps by a Bullmastiff can do to a fence. It is advisable to build your fencing so that the dog can see out. He will soon learn to ignore the less annoying problems if he can see what is going on outside.

The strength of a chain is as strong as its weakest link. This goes for the gate in your fence. It is a waste of time to secure your property with a safe fence only to have a gate swing open at a touch. Never forget that this area is your dog's territory, and he will not take happily to any stranger coming through the gate. Lock it, put up warnings (check locally for the correct wording) and, if necessary, install a bell. Remember, no matter how foolish the interloper may be, you and the whole of the breed fancy will suffer if you are negligent and someone gets hurt.

So now you have his environment safe and secure, what about his sleeping quarters?

If your garden is not particularly big it may serve as the whole dog run. In this case you need only provide the sleeping quarters. If, however, you have more land you may choose to build a dog run within the area to confine your dog when you are out or when you have guests.

In the latter case, pre-stretched panels of fence wire, chain link or other suitable fencing material can easily serve as a run for your dog. Ideally the run should be a minimum of 4m x 1m (12ft x 4ft), sloping, and allowing your dog easy access to water and food when necessary. If he is

Am/Can Ch Garroway N SageHill's Reubon, CGC. Photo: Gail Painter

not going to be in the run for long, a gravel base will keep his muscles in fine trim, and the gravel can be raked level after use. Hygiene is the main consideration here. If your dog stays in the run long enough to produce quantities of faeces, a malodorous environment may result even if pick-up is regular, and gravel is not the best medium. In such cases, a concrete base with a slope of a minimum of 3.5cm per metre (0.5in per lateral foot) is advisable, with a drain on the lower end that takes the waste far away. Such runs are easy to wash and maintain in a hygienic state. One warning here though: long spells on a concrete run will cause your dog's feet to splay, so make sure there is plenty of time for him to relax on grass or on a gravel area to tone up his muscles.

All the indoor considerations apply when considering an outdoor sleeping area. There is also need for a weatherproof covering. The structure should be strong and large enough for the dog to stand up and walk around. He may find it awkward to settle if his muscles are aching and his movements are restricted and will therefore spend a very uncomfortable night trying to relax. The external opening should face away from the prevailing winds with a weatherproof flap to break the wind. Most

Spanish Ch Hilderstone Boss (Photo courtesy of S. Hamnett)

Bullmastiffs eat the flaps sooner or later so it is best to work around this aspect.

Failing this an interior solid panel to deflect any incoming wind will help deter draughts. Draughts and damp are the main concerns. Most Bullmastiffs can put up with cold or heat, but dampness and draughtiness can contribute to the early onset of arthritis. An electric light bulb underneath the floor can sometimes be of value to ward off any such problems. It is not necessary to provide heated quarters but it is kind to keep the damp away. The kennel must be elevated from the ground to minimise dampness and thus decrease the incidence of the ailments that affect dogs when they are allowed to lie on the damp ground.

The approach to the entrance of the kennel should be sloped rather than stepped. Some Bullmastiffs refuse to pick up their feet properly when stepping into their kennel and repeatedly bump their pastern joints on the step. In time this produces an ossial contusion, or bruising of the bone, which shows as a rather ugly, calcified lump on the pastern joint. This is not a pretty sight and will most certainly be disadvantageous to your dog in any show ring.

Outdoor bedding can take the form of straw or hay. Either will keep him warm at night and keep his coat clean and shining. It should be cleaned out weekly to prevent flea infestation.

Do not leave excess food outside as this will attract flies. Provide water in a bucket, or you can buy a mechanism that fits the garden tap and releases water only when licked. Placing both food and water utensils at chest height allows your dog to eat standing up and stretches his muscles in the right direction. To bend the neck right down and eat at the same time does not do much for digestion or the dog's neck muscles. Reaching up to eat will help him to develop strong pastern muscles and good neck musculature.

You now have the right environment, the right house, the right bedding and the right eating methods. By the time you have read this far you know all the ways to enjoy the company of your Bullmastiff.

Make the most of him while he is a puppy; he will soon be grown up. Watch him grow and learn together how to coexist in a way that is right for both of you and for everyone else around him. When he grows up perhaps you will think of breeding, showing or both. Well, you have gone much further than you thought you would at one stage, so why not look a little further still? The next steps are no more frightening or confusing than the ones you have just taken. Remember when you thought that was a big step? By this time you are a fully-fledged Bullmastiff fancier. So read on!

CHAPTER SIX

Training

Why, you may ask, does there have to be a section on training so soon after selecting your puppy? Everyone knows that sooner or later a dog has to be trained. Why not wait until later?

The cute little Bullmastiff puppy you just brought home is more than likely the whole centre of attention at the moment. Well, I cannot stress too many times that this little bundle of fun, probably about 9kg (20lb) at present, is going to be gaining weight at about 4.5kg (10lb) a month for the first year. At the tender age of nine months he will weigh about 40kg (90lb); and at one year will be well over 45kg (100lb). Time will pass quickly and you should understand one thing clearly: if at the age of one year you cannot control this large dog with commands to which he will respond, the chances are you will not be able to do it physically. This puppy will be stronger at one year of age than most of your family. Do not wait until then to find you have made a big mistake. No one likes a badly behaved dog, especially when he is bigger than everything else around him.

Start training your puppy as soon as he arrives home. This does not mean you have to take him outside immediately for formal obedience training. More realistically, his initial training will take the form of correction of his responses to new experiences, which will give the puppy paws-on experience.

The Social conscience has changed remarkably since my previoius book in 1999. In that book I outlined many forms of training, including obedience, protection etc. Since that time, ideas and protocols have changed so much in different countries, especially in reference to Breed Specific Legistlation (BSL) that I would now refer you to an experienced trainer in your locality. Check the credentials carefully and follow his/her instructions. In this book, I will refer only to the training needed for showing. This remains generally constant in most countries in which this book will be seen.

Showing

How do you feel about taking your dog into the ring and winning his championship? Most people shy away and quickly decline this invitation on grounds of inexperience and ignorance of proceedings. Well, now you will have no excuse. Read the following and be prepared to venture out into the spotlight.

Spotlight? No, not really. The first sensible thing to remember is the show is not for you; it is for your dog. Many novices work up a nervous condition while waiting outside the ring and are almost wrecks before the proceedings begin. Let me tell you as a judge, you are not the important part of the partnership entering the ring; your dog is. When your number is called the eyes of the judge and the public are watching what is at the end of the leash: the bottom end. Once you can register this through your trembling the fright will be gone. To be honest, after you have paid your entry fee and your travel costs to the show plus, perhaps, your overnight stay you have approximately two minutes in which to show the judge the mettle of your dog. If you are placed anywhere other than Best of Breed, or Best Puppy in Breed, your time is over until the next show. The point to be made here is that in those two minutes you will be fully occupied showing off every part of your dog's conformation in an effort to convince the judge you have the best dog. In fact you will be working so hard you will not have time to reflect on whether your hair is a mess or you are handling correctly. In that two minutes you will be working with every ounce of energy on the dog and, if you are doing it well, all eyes will be on the dog, not you. Remember that!

I am sure you will have butterflies the first show; everyone does. Once you realise that you have paid for your time and you are going to get your money's worth, the time will be over: hopefully you have won, and it was not really all that bad, was it? The next show will be 10 times easier.

Always remember when you enter the show ring that it is a show, and the operative word is 'show'. You could have a superior dog to your competitor, but if you handle poorly and he does it well, who will come out with the ribbon?

The ring, actually a square, is approximately 12m x 12m (40ft x 40ft). This ring is the domain and kingdom of the judge. While you are in the ring, remember this and pay attention to the judge's and steward's instructions. The judge will always tell you what he wants and will ask you to do certain things for reasons of his own to pick the best dog. A brief visit to the ring before your breed is due to be shown will give you a good idea of the judge's method of operation and help you to avoid going in unaware of his ring procedure.

The steward will call you to the edge of the ring just before you are due to go in. It is your responsibility to be waiting at the entrance; the steward will not go looking for you. If you are not there you could be marked absent and lose your chance to show that day. Wait quietly until the steward calls your number and pay attention when he tells you where to go in the ring. Always remember: in the time you are in the ring you must do all you can to present the best of your dog to the judge. Never place yourself between the dog and the judge; make sure you manoeuvre yourself into a position on the opposing side of your dog to the judge. If he looks up and sees something about your dog that catches his eye it will leave a lasting impression.

A typical procedure will be for the judge to ask all the exhibitors to gait their dogs around the ring for him to see the relative movements. Following this usually is a detailed inspection of each dog, then an individual gaiting so each dog's movement can be studied. After completing this step the judge will make his selection of the best dog. Depending on the country in which the dog is shown the sequence of placement and awards will differ. The ultimate award is to determine the best example of the breed shown, in this case the best Bullmastiff. The best Bullmastiff will then be shown against other best dogs in the Working Group (Akitas, Malamutes and others). The best dog from this Group selection will be shown against the best dogs from the other groups (for example, best herding dog and best sporting dog). The final award is that of the Best in Show (BIS). Depending on the country of exhibition, the winning dog gains points at each level. These are collated over the year to determine the best dog at breed and group level and the dog's standing overall compared to all the other dogs shown in the country for that year.

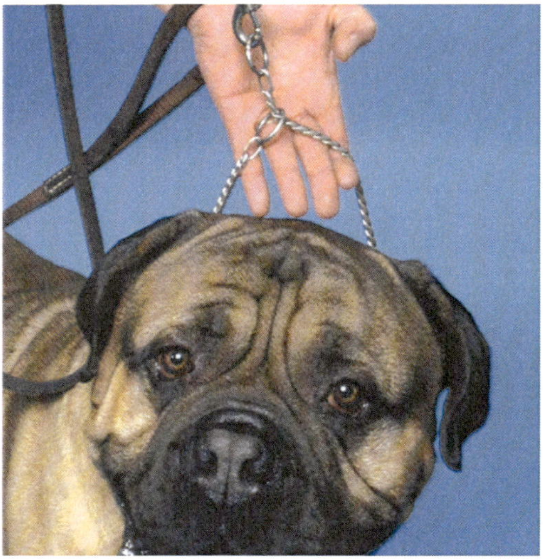
The correct way to put on a choke chain.

This is a simplification of the whole procedure but serves to explain the general concept of conformation showing. For more information contact your local show Secretary or Kennel Club.

While in the ring you will be asked to complete certain procedures, and words may be used that you have not heard before. To assist you as a novice the following may be of help.

Gait

This refers to moving your dog. A Bullmastiff should be moved as fast as is necessary to show his best movement: not walking or galloping, not too fast, not too slow. Practice will tell you which is the best speed for your dog. Do not judge your gait speed by others around you. Your dog's best gaiting speed will depend on his conformation. Use a video, full length mirror or have an experienced friend watch you to guage the most appropriate speeed to show off your dog.

Before you attend your first championship point show it is a good idea to attend one of the many sanction or puppy matches arranged by local dog clubs. These practice shows are a good introduction for young puppies and novices alike to the world of showing. The atmosphere at these shows is much less competitive and those

Eng Ch Licassa Captain Archembeau (Photo courtesy C. Quantrill)

attending are more than willing to give tips and advice to the newcomer.

Stack

'Stack' is the term used when the dog is positioned in his best stance to show off his conformation. A Bullmastiff should stand 'four square'. This means all of his four legs support his body as if they were the legs of a table.

Moving the Bullmastiff.

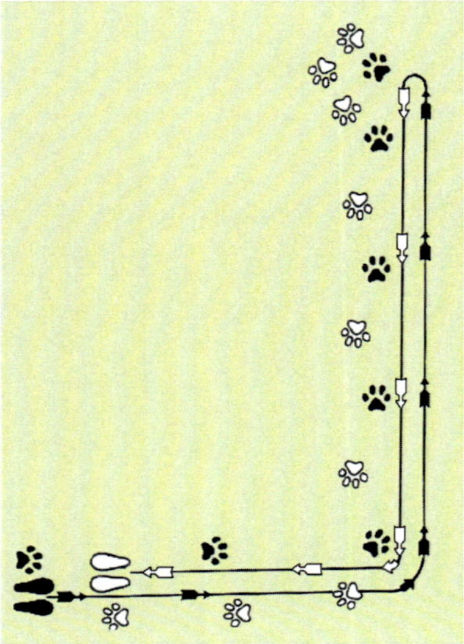

L pattern (involving change of lead hand to keep dog between you and judge at all times).

The front legs should be vertical and placed beneath his shoulders so that he displays his broad chest well and supports his upper body fully. If you move his legs too far forward he will resemble a rocking horse, and will also throw his forequarter weight backwards instead of over his front legs, causing his back to dip. A strong, straight top line is important. His back feet should be placed in such a position as to give him a good, straight top line, and preferably vertical hocks. The positioning of his back feet will depend on the precise amount of angulation in his stifle (knee) and the length of his back. Too much angulation will often necessitate the back legs being placed so far back to give the correct top line that the dog will appear long backed.

The head should be held up in

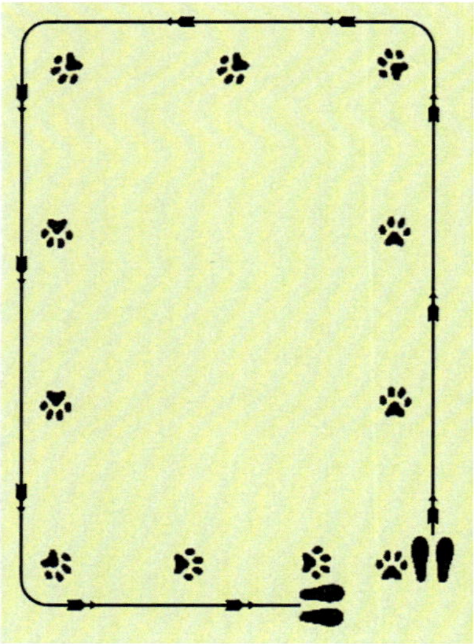

Using the whole ring - including the corners - to move your dog.

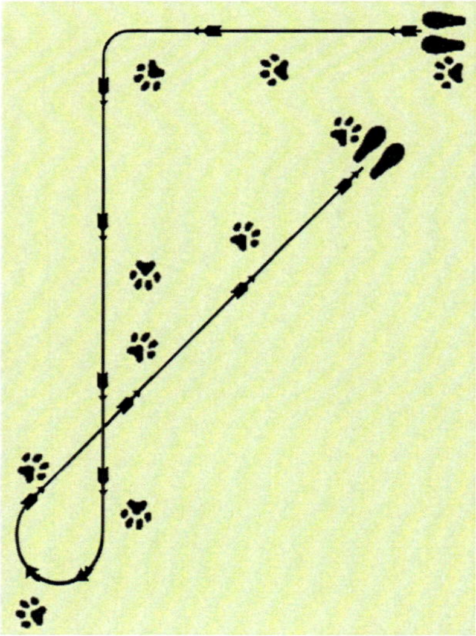

The Triangle.

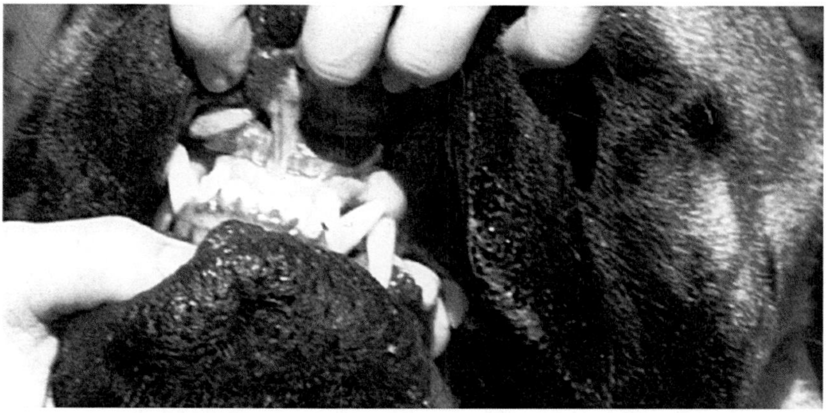

Showing the teeth for the judge's inspection. Be sure to expose clearly all the incisors and canines. Wide canines are a good indication of broadness of muzzle, so don't miss the opportunity to show this to your judge.

such a manner as to show off his expression, with ears forward and a good arch of neck. This last action can be enhanced by pulling up on the choker collar at the same time as pressing down on the withers area. Be sure the choker collar is positioned under his chin in a manner that does not collect up the extra skin and makes your dog look as if he has double chins.

Examination

The judge comes towards you to examine your dog. If you have done your practice correctly your dog should stand still. Younger dogs are excused a little fidgeting but older dogs are expected to allow examination without fuss. Remember, show your dog, not your arm or jacket or skirt. Keep yourself out of view of the judge no matter what it takes to do so.

The judge will normally ask to see the dog's teeth, or bite. At this point you are expected to open the dog's mouth to show the front teeth and their respective bite. Some judges will do this themselves but generally they will ask you. Some Bullmastiffs have a very thick pad of skin at the front of their bottom lip so flashing the teeth is not easy. As you show the teeth you must also maintain the dog in a stationary position, so be sure you have practised well before going in front of a judge. It is wise to carry a piece of cloth in a handy pocket so that when you have shown the teeth you can quickly and unobtrusively wipe away any saliva on the dog's face or your hands. When the judge has examined the head he will examine the rest of the dog and you will have to move away from the side of your dog for him to do this. To maintain control over your dog hold the head tightly. This will stop a nervous or inquisitive dog from turning his head to interfere with the judge's examination. At the same time you can control the balance of the dog by deftly manoeuvring the head to prejudice the weight positioning of the dog over his feet and keep him standing as he is. Practice will show you how to induce the dog to move parts of his body as you wish, using his head as a remote control device. This will keep the dog in a standing, stationary, show position for the judge's examination. Many judges take one last look before moving on to the next dog so do not relax too soon.

Moving your dog

This is when you will be asked to move the dog individually. This is your moment to shine, so listen carefully to what the judge asks you to do. You should have practised the following movements at home and you can also watch other exhibitors on the day to see what they do.

The Triangle

This is a common movement in which the dog is moved from the judge directly down the side of the ring. At the first corner he is moved to the next corner, at right angles to the initial movement. The dog is then turned to come directly back to the judge. In such a large breed as the Bullmastiff, it is accepted protocol to use your body as a pivot point to turn the dog at the second corner. Although this blocks the view of the dog momentarily, doing a full turn in insufficient space can look clumsy and detract from your dog's gait. When you approach the judge do not bowl him over with a runaway dog. As you near him, the judge may signal for you to stop. This is your cue to stop your dog close to him in a superb show stance. This takes a little practice but it is very impressive if done nicely.

The 'L'

This movement is not liked by many handlers but is occasionally asked for by judges. The dog is moved as in the first two movements of the triangle but at the far corner, instead of moving directly to the judge, the steps are retraced. The trick in this is to teach your dog that at the about turn he will be coming back on the other side of you from that to which he has become accustomed. He will have to learn that he is expected to continue on this other side until he returns to the first corner, at which time he will pass in front of you onto his accustomed side to complete the remainder of the procedure. Although this is not asked for too many times you should practise it just in case. Remember: do not put yourself between the dog and the judge.

Using The Whole Ring

After the individual examination the judging is usually completed by the judge asking you to move your dog around the ring to the end of the line. At this time keep your eye on the judge, have your dog looking his best, and listen carefully for any instructions. If you are placed you will go into line by the position markers. If you are not, praise your dog so he knows that he has done well and leave the ring quietly and graciously. A congratulatory comment to the winner on the way out would be good etiquette.

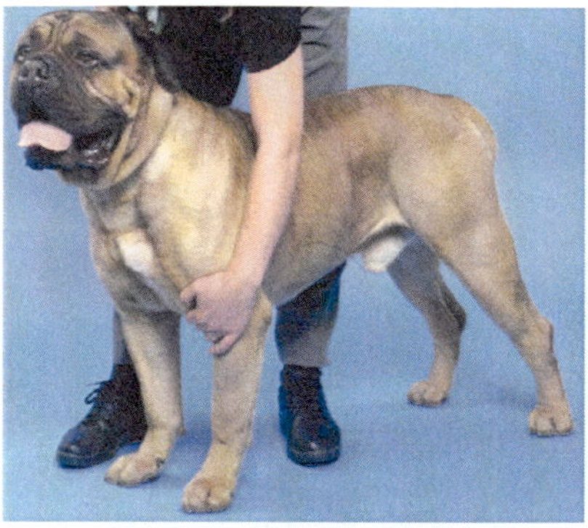

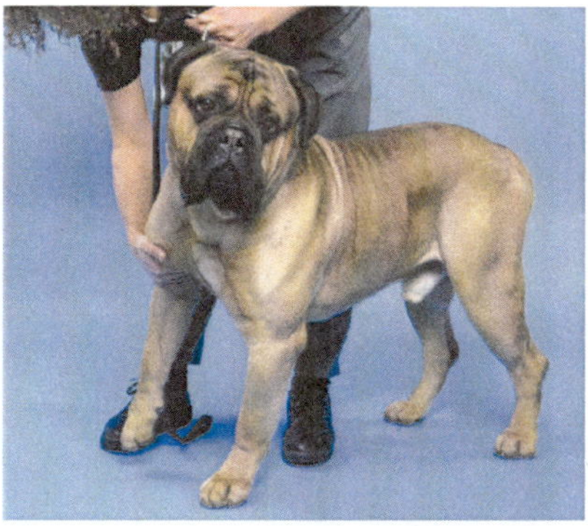

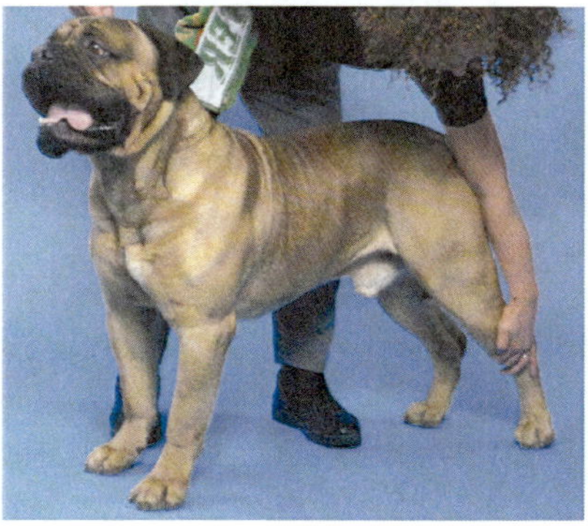

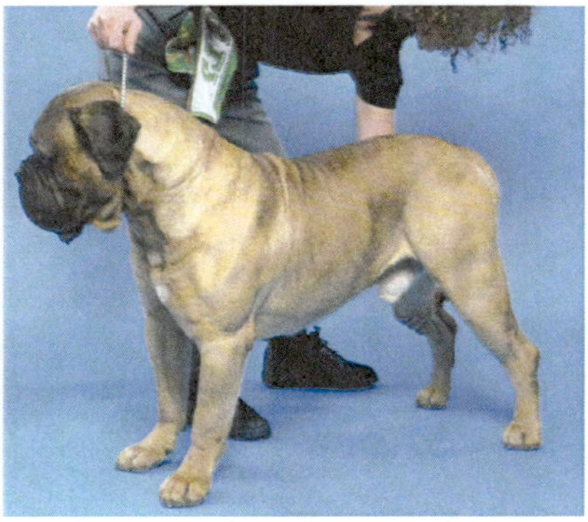

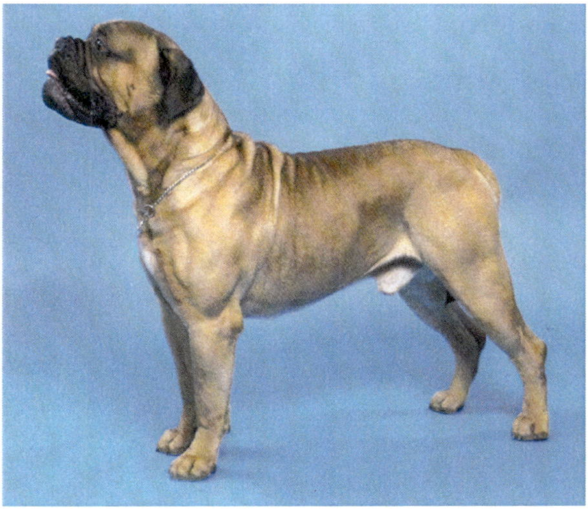

Stacking the dog for the judge.

Top left: Set the left front leg first by grasping the elbow (never the foot). This is the first part of the dog that the judge will see, so position it first. **Top right:** Move the right front, again by the elbow. This allows the dog's weight to balance over the leg. **Centre left:** Holding the head up with a firm hand on the collar to prevent the dog moving out of the stack on the front, set the outside back leg by grasping the hock. If the judge were to look at your dog now, he is complete enough in the stack. **Centre right:** The final setting of the dog by adjusting the inside back hock. This can also be used to adjust the dog if he is leaning in the wrong direction or his topline is incorrect. **Bottom:** A beautifully stacked dog.

CHAPTER SEVEN

Breeding

If your knowledge of Bullmastiffs is limited and you have not seen other Bullmastiffs, take a trip to another area and familiarise yourself. Video cameras can sometimes save you the cost of a trip if the fancier you choose to contact is co-operative.

Take time to research honestly long before you have need of a mate for your dog. One of the best people to talk to is the breeder of your own dog. Since you bought your Bullmastiff from the breeder because you liked it better than the others you saw, the chances are that you appreciated your breeder's programme. He will be knowledgeable about his dogs' lines and the prepotencies of your dog and will recommend a mate. He can tell you what you might expect in your litter.

Mating – The Easy Way

Like everything else in life, there is an easy way and a hard way. Considering the size, weight, and disposition of this large breed it is not hard to see it could be quite problematic trying to manoeuvre two very large dogs, sometimes as big as their owners, into cooperating in a way that might not be agreeable to them at that particular time, for whatever reasons. The attempt can result in two very tired handlers full of frustration, and no chance of conception in sight. The following section provides the novice with a proven and tried method of breeding Bullmastiffs in a way known to be successful and relatively easy. As the proverb says: 'When all else fails, read these instructions'.

The only aim in mating is to allow the semen of the male to fertilise the ova of the female. No matter how you put it the outcome is the same the whole world over and in every culture. The action is as basic as life itself and anyone engaging in this age-old ritual has to accept this fact before proceeding any further. To this end the following chapter is explicit, comprehensive and explains everything you wanted to know about canine sex but were afraid to ask.

There are two ways of connecting the semen to the ova successfully: artificially, otherwise known as artificial insemination (AI), and the natural, physical way. The only right way is the way that results in conception; the choice of method will depend on the owner of the bitch or the agreement of contract between the owners of the two dogs involved.

Long before either method is used the owner of the bitch should have determined within a reasonable time when the bitch is due to come into heat. Some bitches show a lot of swelling and discolouration of the vulva when heat approaches, others can be so discreet that, unless the owner is watching, the bitch can sneak in and out of heat and not give her secret away. The usual signs of heat are fussiness, during which the bitch licks and cleans herself profusely, and the need to urinate often. However, instead of stooping and emptying her bladder normally, the bitch mimics the male action and leaves little drops everywhere to attract males. She will inevitably leave blood spots around. Some bitches show a lot, some very little, so beware of being fooled by a bitch that appears not to be in heat.

Eng Ch Licassa Golden Grace (Photo courtesy C. Quantrill)

As soon as this starts it will be as well to pay a visit to your veterinary surgeon. Unless you know your bitch well you may not be able to catch the first day of oestrus accurately. It is very important to determine the day of ovulation or your efforts at breeding will be wasted. The day of ovulation varies from dog to dog and the only way to be sure of it the first time is to study cells from your bitch's uterus that have been discharged by her as she enters her heat period. Your vet will take a vaginal smear and stain and check it under the microscope to see how far into the heat she is.

Artificial Insemination

Many breeders prefer this approach all the time as it avoids physical contact and transmission of many diseases, and allows the breeder to determine the time and the quality and amount of sperm, and to have control of the whole procedure.

Prior to any interaction between the two candidates clinical protocol must be observed. The genital areas of both animals must be cleaned with an antiseptic solution to avoid the cross-transmission of bacterial infections or any other communicable diseases.

Some males need the presence of the female to initiate erection. If this is so allow the male to acquaint himself with the rear end of the female and the odorous discharge will bring his attention into line..

Once erection is accomplished the semen will soon flow, the male's pulsations also occurring at 0.8 per second. If the penis is grasped at the base behind the bulbous area this action will simulate the muscular action of the female and maintain erection. Experience and scrutiny will tell the operator when it is time to finish collection of the semen. The first 30–60 seconds of emission usually contain old and inactive semen. The second portion (times may overlap) at approximately 50–80 seconds is the sample that will contain the necessary motile semen. After that, the ejaculated fluid is that of lubricant, mostly from the prostate gland and almost clear in colour in comparison to the whiter, denser colour of the true semen.

The collection vessel can be anything from a large medical syringe to a glass sterilised beforehand and allowed to come to room temperature before use, assuming room temperature is about 24°C (75°F). Once collected the semen will cool quickly and must be administered to the female as soon as possible. Do not bang the vessel as canine semen is very fragile and a bump can kill your sample and make any further action that time futile. At this time some breeders prefer to check the motility and count of the sample by using a slide and a small droplet from the vessel to assure themselves all is well with the male if the bitch does not conceive.

For a Bullmastiff an open-ended catheter similar to the kind used for horses or cows is ideal for depositing the semen. Administering is made easier if the catheter is cut to approximately 20cm (8in) and the end is

Fi & Lv & Am & Ru & By & Ru Gr Ch Ru JCH JWW-09 UA CH V-10 BYW-09 BALTW-10 Lemabull Pass The Game To Antallis - photo credit: Riikka Holappa

flamed to round it and remove any straight or rough edges. To this attach a 20cc syringe and carefully withdraw the sample from the vessel. A good sample to give a reasonable chance of conception would be 10–15cc. Do not withdraw the plunger of the syringe any further when all the sample has been removed from the vessel. One thing not required in the vagina is air.

Be sure you have enough assistance to prevent the bitch's head from turning towards you for obvious reasons, and have someone hold her tail out of the way. The bitch's vagina does not connect with the outside world in a straight continuous line so be prepared for this. As you enter the catheter into the vulva you will be aware that the vagina rises slightly and is sometimes partially blocked by a flap of membrane. Careful manoeuvring of the catheter will negotiate this membrane and the bend in the vagina and the catheter can then be inserted fully.

If the vagina seems resistant to the insertion movements or you believe you have reached the furthest point of deposition, slightly withdraw the catheter and eject a small quantity of the semen. If the problem is lubrication the small emission will assist the continuing procedure; if not you will know that the point of deposition has been reached. Sometimes when the catheter goes easily the end wall of the vagina is soon reached. However, when the plunger is depressed, a resistance is noticed due to the fact that the soft tissue at the end of the vagina has completely sealed off the end of the catheter. Then, as with the lubrication problem, a slight

withdrawal will cure the situation and the plunger can be depressed.

Now is the important time of deposition. Depress the plunger slowly and evenly until the syringe is empty. If you withdraw the catheter at this time you will siphon out quite a large amount of the semen by the displacement effect of the catheter. Therefore remove the syringe from the catheter and quickly place your thumb over the open end of the catheter to avoid leakage, withdraw the plunger of the syringe about 2cc and re-connect to the catheter. Remembering that you do not want air in the vagina, depress the syringe plunger slowly at the same time as you withdraw the syringe and catheter from the vagina. This allows the maximum amount of semen to stay where it should with the minimum loss. In case the bitch coughs, barks, or moves suddenly pinch the lips of the vulva together to avoid loss of semen and possible ruination of your AI. If it is possible try to raise the rear end of the bitch off the floor by whatever method is available for approximately five minutes.

If you can negotiate the little finger of the hand through the lips of the vulva and apply pressure to the bitch's clitoris, the natural pulsation of 0.8 per second can be produced in the vaginal sphincter muscle, assisting the semen along its natural course. Do not allow the bitch to urinate for 20 minutes.

This concludes the breeding by AI. Depending on the arrangement between the two owners of the parent dogs, this may be all that's involved. Further breedings will depend on the ambient breeding protocol or contract terms.

Natural Breeding

Natural breeding is very aclinical. It presents a very different scene from AI, when all genital contact areas such as vulva and penis sheath are clean and comparatively sterile and free from transmissible infection. For the purpose of this section, we will assume that both bitch and dog are novices at breeding.

The genital areas of both dogs should be checked for cleanliness. If in doubt wash the genitals with an aseptic solution.

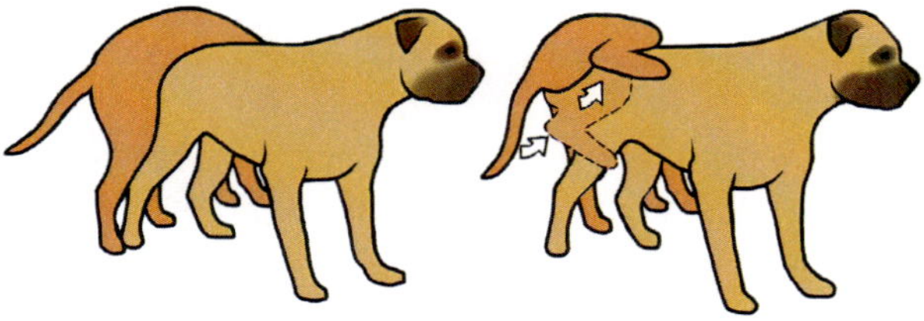

Some male dogs' senses are very acute and the presence of a bitch in heat is obvious to them. However, some bitches, no matter how much in heat, need to check out the sex of the dog approaching them. Both dogs should be secure on leads to allow a sensory introduction on both their parts. It will serve to assure the bitch that this really is a male approaching her, and it will heighten the male's sexual acuity. Many males would be satisfied with a headlong rush and rape at first sight. Such a blundering approach will only serve to scare or intimidate a nervous bitch into total refusal to mate. An experienced bitch will know what to expect and often put up with much more roughness than a maiden bitch. If not controlled by the handler, inexperienced males will often rush at the bitch too quickly and ejaculate prematurely, thus

Fi Ch Big Ida Red-Like-Copper (10 years old !) - photo credit: Riikka Holappa

ruining all chances of a successful mating. After numerous breedings the handlers of the bitch and dog both know what to expect and so the necessary adjustments to control can be made to suit the occasion.

Chat Raff 5/$20 Some breeders like to allow their dogs to run around and get to know each other before actual mating starts. Once again this is fine if you know your dogs well. However, if the male gets too amorous too soon for the bitch's liking the romantic frolic can soon turn sour. Depending on the mood of the bitch, this can be so quick and sudden that it may be impossible to prevent this. The way your Bullmastiff reacts under such conditions may show you a side of your dog you have not hitherto encountered in your gentle family pet.

Be prepared and be safe; do not let your dog or yourself get bitten because of romantic reversions. Keep your dog on the lead even when allowing the pair to flirt. This way if courtship takes a wrong turn you can intervene before it gets serious and the mating will not be affected. For the safety of the male who will be preoccupied in mounting the female without any thought for his personal safety, the female's head should be held tightly forward. This prevents her turning and biting the male's face should she not appreciate his physical endeavours. If her head is held tightly it will also ensure her body stays in line with her head. In case she does happen to swing around it is useful to have a third party present to move her back into position.

The male should be allowed to approach her slowly, not with a rush; careful manipulation with the lead will produce this effect. The male will mount from the back and commence the hip movement associated with copulation. At this point the movement is voluntary and controlled and he may dismount and restart more than once. At this time the tip of the penis has not come into contact with the vulva and remains quite small. However, once the end of the penis has encountered the vulva opening, involuntary muscular thrusts will occur as the vulva creates pressure on the penis. It is of the greatest importance that the male's genitals are as close to the female's as possible at this point to ensure maximum penetration. In a novice dog that is too far from the female it may be necessary for the handler to assist quickly by pushing the rear end of the dog closer to the female with a timely forward movement of his knee.

This will ensure the penetration necessary to place the bulbous area inside the female vaginal sphincter muscle. This action is necessary to ensure a tie. If the bulbous area of the penis enlarges outside the sphincter muscle the bitch may be able to prevent his total withdrawal by gripping his penis, but failure to tie will lead ultimately to the dog's premature withdrawal and possible failure of the mating and conception. The importance of this physical closeness at the time of the thrusting cannot be stressed enough. If the male is a little nervous and becomes frustrated when no penetration is achieved, his handler may need to assist by gently guiding the male's penis to the entrance of the vulva.

Once physical contact is made the natural reactions will take over.

To avoid potential problems it is wiser to turn the dogs so they are end to end. The secret in the turning at this point is not the elbow but the male's stifle, or knee. If he has dropped down onto her right it is his left stifle (knee) you will be manipulating. Bend the male's stifle by grasping the hock and push the knee over the female's back and at the same time pull his head in the opposite direction to the female's. The leg will naturally drop down and, with a little manoeuvring, the dogs will be end to end. At delicate moments you may hear a little complaining by the female, but as long as you move slowly and take care that their tails are out of the way, no harm will come to either.

During the tie either or both dogs may appear to lose interest in the proceedings and attempt to dissolve the partnership. Sometimes

Bullgrin's Kanga-Roo - Photo Credit: Riikka Holappa

the female will try to sit down, or the male to walk off. To avoid physical damage to either, both handlers should make themselves comfortable on stools and hold the dogs in the end-to-end position. The dogs should be supervised in this fashion until the tie is over.

Once the tie is over the male will disconnect from the female and be more interested in his toiletries than in the female, who will be glad to be taken away quietly. With a little self cleaning the male's penis should resume normal proportions and withdraw safely to the protection of its sheath. After the tie has broken the male will attend to himself, then look for a drink of water and a place to rest. This rest is important for both animals if healthy breeding stock is to be maintained. Fewer problems of

stress and weight maintenance will be noticed if the two animals involved are housed well away from each other during the breeding time.

Care of the Bitch after Mating

Your bitch has just been mated and you are hopeful of a litter. How you handle the female in the next two months will decide just how successful that is to be.

After the mating take your female away and put her somewhere peaceful and, if possible, private. You need to keep her quiet and subdued; any undue excitement such as meeting another bitch

face to face or a cat that needs to be investigated can ruin your chances of success.

A confined area such as a crate is preferable and be sure she does not urinate for at least 20 minutes. The urge in female dogs in oestrus to do this as an advertisement to males is extremely strong. If she does this after mating the siphoning action can cause her to lose all the valuable semen you have just spent time acquiring. A quiet time for your bitch will be most suitable no matter how long you think fertilisation takes.

If she has conceived, physical changes soon start to show. Appetite is often the first indicator: all of a sudden the food intake increases dramatically. This is a good sign, but do not let your dog eat gluttonously and become overweight, as this will affect the correct working of other organs.

The nipples of an unbred bitch are usually flat and pinched. After breeding, hormone activity tends to swell the nipples so that they are plump and pink after conception, usually showing a difference the

Se Ch Maxinice Kirstey A- Photo Credit: Peter Pettison

Bullberry Queniva - Photo Credit: Riikka Holappa

day after mating. In the latter weeks take great care to make sure she does not jump up or down on anything, causing her to stretch the abdominal area of her body. This can cause severe movement of the puppies in the uterus horns and problems at birth. As the pressure mounts within her be aware that the pressure on her bladder means she needs to urinate frequently, and do not get impatient as she asks to go outside yet again.

The milk glands on the female's underside will begin to show like corded ropes, and traces of milk may become evident if the nipples are squeezed. As she gets heavier and more cumbersome, walking and general manoeuvring will become an effort, so do not hurry her. Be prepared to make allowances. She is big, heavy, often irritated, and probably wishing it was all over.

Although she is gravid, most fanciers would be amazed at the rate of response this rather turgid female can muster when she or her family are threatened. There is nothing more awesome than an almost full-term female Bullmastiff coming around in a defensive rush, so make sure she does not have to respond like this.

Whelping to Weaning

The Bullmastiff bitch becomes a very cumbersome and ungainly animal as the day approaches for her to whelp the pups. Birth usually occurs approximately 63 days after conception, although this can alter by a few days depending on the individual dog. If you are unsure a quick visit to your vet at about the 60-day mark may better prepare you for the actual day.

Because bitches seem to choose the most inadequate places in which to have puppies it is better for man and beast if your female is confined to a whelping box for the duration of the birth and a short while afterwards. Most pets object to being confined in one area when they are used to being with members of the family all the time; however for the benefit of the puppies, her own safety, and control of the situation, a whelping box is the more suitable alternative to chaos.

The whelping box

The most useful type of whelping box serves initially as a whelping area and afterwards as a puppy box until the puppies are about four weeks old. In dimensions it is 120cm x 120cm (4ft x 4ft). A piece of plywood raised off the floor serves well, the raised area preventing cold or dampness coming up through the bottom. It is often better to leave this 'floor' unfinished except for the scantiest covering of newspaper. It should either be natural wood or wood painted in such a way that there will be adequate traction for the puppies. This avoids any covering being piled up and perhaps a puppy suffocating as a result of a well-meaning mother nesting and inadvertently covering it over. A newspaper covering is cheap and convenient, and any soiled material can be quickly removed as events proceed. The sides of the whelping box are made from a full piece of 120cm x 240cm (4ft x 8ft) plywood cut into four strips, each 60cm x 120cm (2ft x 4ft). These strips form the walls of the whelping box on three sides. On the fourth side, the strip is cut again to give two pieces of plywood 30cm x 120cm (1ft x 4ft). These two pieces are hinged to each other on the 120cm edge and attached on one of the 120cm edges to the floor on the partially completed whelping box. The hinged part that is free allows one side to be lowered to allow the bitch to come and go as her owner desires. During times of complete confinement or whelping, the hinged part can be raised and the whelping box made secure.

A most important part of the whelping equipment is the heat lamp. This can take the form of a chick brooder bulb with a protective safety cage around it or a heating panel as used in pig rearing. Either can be used successfully to create a floor temperature of 30°C (85°F) for the first week. This allows the puppies to stay warm enough to ward off herpes, pneumonia, or any other infection to which they may be vulnerable when the mother is not present to keep them at the right temperature. For the first days of life the puppies rely on you and your heating lamp, or their mother, to control their body temperature; their natural thermostats will not be functioning yet. This temperature can be gradually lowered to 24°C (75°F) after a week. This extra thought will allow the mother a little freedom from her maternal chores as the pups will not immediately miss her when she leaves the box and takes her body heat with her. If the heat is aimed in such a way as to cover only one half of the whelping box the mother will often lie out of the heat path, but the puppies will be snug and warm.

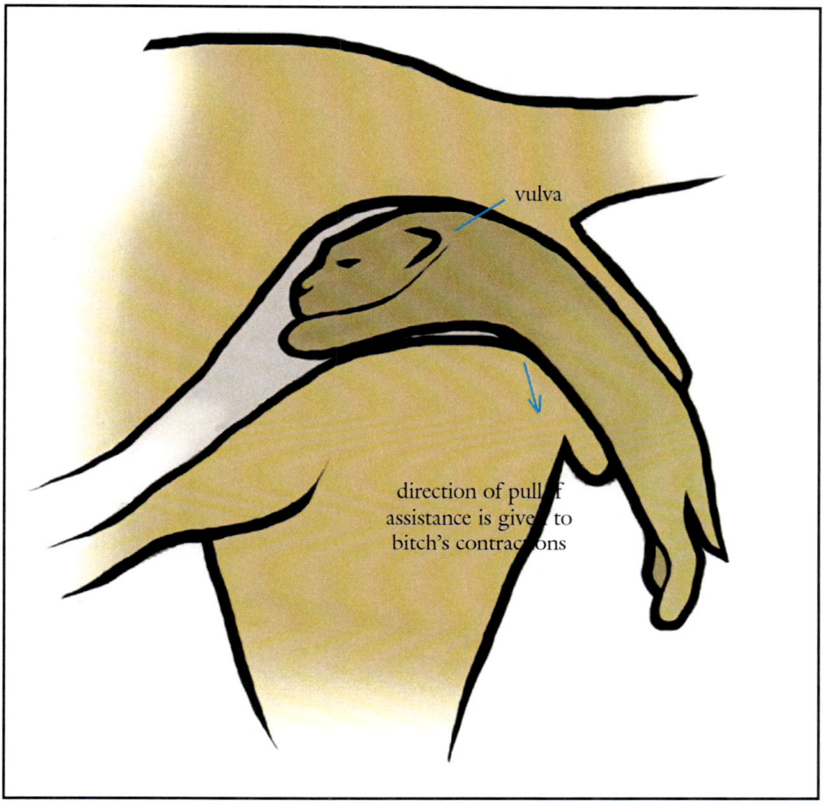

Assisting the bitch during a breach birth.

One final structure in the whelping box and everything is ready: this is the crush rail. During whelping, and just after, the presence of puppies may not be obvious or of concern to a first-time mother. Occasionally the bitch will lie down suddenly and onto the puppies. After a short while she learns to slide down and push any puppies in the way out of her lying area, so causing no harm. However, in the early days precautions have to be taken to ensure the litter's safety. The crush rail consists of a wooden rail 5cm x 5cm (2in x 2in) running around the inside of the whelping box approximately 15cm (6in) off the floor and 30cm (12in) from the walls. This can be further enhanced by blocking out the corners in the box and presenting a floor area that will not allow puppies to become squashed into any corner but always in a position to claim mother's attention. In the first few days of life puppies react to stimulus such as heat and pain by crying, but cannot move away, so all possibilities have to be considered in designing the whelping box.

It helps if the whelping box becomes the bitch's home about two weeks before the litter is due. This overcomes her objections in plenty of time and allows her to settle down to normal living before the babies

Barbara Shoneck's High Hill's Sugar 'n' Spice with her first litter.

arrive. Place the whelping box in a quiet, well lit, warm, draught-free area where she can have privacy when the time comes but also in a position that gives you easy access when you want.

Labour

Prior to whelping, the bitch indulges in a great deal of excessive action: frantic nest building, asking to go out to urinate, panting, and general restlessness. A sure sign that puppies are imminent is the failure to eat her meal. Up to this time she usually eats ravenously but the day of the birth most mothers-to-be cover over their meal and want no part of iit. This is the time to prepare a small puppy-holding box and line it with a clean towel and a heating pad. Set the heat control on low. If the puppy becomes too hot his feet and abdomen will go bright pink or purple. The puppies will cry if they get too cold, but too much heat may result in brain damage and a dead puppy.

Whelping

As the birth begins, strong muscular contractions will be seen in the stomach area. There will be some false starts when she will stop straining and sleep or look around uninterestedly. However, once the serious pushing begins, puppies are on the way. Do not allow her to strain and strain when nothing seems to be happening, certainly for no more than three hours. If your dog is in obvious distress contact your vet. It is a good idea to have pre-warned him or her of your possible middle-of-the-night appeal.

In most cases a puppy will appear head first. Do not be distressed if you see your puppy appearing bottom first (breach birth). This is quite common in this breed and most bitches have little problem delivering a breach. Should the puppy be an exceptionally big one and the breach

Aust Ch Treebrook Sweet Eldar (Photo courtesy B. & K. Marion)

presentation render whelping even more difficult, you may have to help. With clean hands, preferably washed in a clinical soap, or failing that with a clean piece of cloth, grasp the rear legs of the half-born puppy. As you feel the mother contract and push, pull gently but firmly. You will be very aware when this happens once you have hold of the puppy. When the bitch stops straining, you stop pulling. Do not try to pull the puppy out between contractions; go with the flow.

Problems like this do not occur too often and usually you can sit and just watch. Depending when the placenta actually detaches, the puppy may have sufficient oxygen to maintain him until the mother breaks the membrane and clears the airways. Sometimes a new mother is confused as to what to do first. Lost time in clearing the membrane may lose you a puppy so reach over and break the membrane around the mouth of the puppy with your fingers; it is very important to get that first breath as soon as possible. The rush of fluid usually stimulates the mother to react and her vigorous licking and pushing stimulates the puppy to breathe and wriggle, hence causing more breathing. Sometimes a mother will be so concerned at removing the afterbirth from herself or the puppy, she will momentarily forget the puppy. The whole point of this exercise is to end up with a live litter and this procedure ensures live puppies regardless of your bitch's attitude. A piece of dry cloth will help you grasp the puppy.

Once the puppy is fully born, quietly reach over and snip the umbilical cord with sharp surgical (round nosed) scissors about 1 inch from the pup's stomach and deftly remove the puppy. The bitch will often be so preoccupied with her toiletries she will not notice. Quickly slip some thread around the severed cord and tie tightly about 1.25cm (0.5in) from the puppy's abdomen, sealing off the umbilical. Now comes the tricky part. Hold the puppy in your two hands so that your index fingers run along the sides of the puppy's mouth and the finger tips are just inside the mouth. Holding this package very tightly raise the puppy above your head and bring your arms down as fast as you can without letting go of your charge. The resultant centrifugal force of this action will eject all of the fluid out of the puppy's lungs and throat and ensure a clear airway.

Photo Credit:
Riikka Holappa

C.I.B Pohj & Fin & Se & No Ch W-05 BullCastle's Red Baron

Some people do not like to take the centrifugal approach except in an emergency.

These actions will cause the puppy to cry out, and sometimes the mother becomes very upset with the person causing this apparent harm to her baby. For this reason you must be ready to return the puppy to his mother quickly. If you present the puppy towards the bitch with your hands behind and under it she will be so glad to see her pup she will forget the cry of distress and be only too pleased to get her baby back.

At this time the bitch will be lavishing all kinds of motherly love on her pup in the form of licking, cleaning, general cleaning-up and eating the afterbirth. If the mother is not too lavish with her licks of life, help out by briskly rubbing the pup's stomach and lung area with a wet, rough face cloth (a dry one burns the skin because of the friction). As soon as you can, make sure the puppy nurses, even if you have to force an unwilling mouth open and over a nipple. It is of extreme importance that the puppy has a measure of the colostrum in the first milk, which passes the bitch's immunity to the pup. Once the puppy has nursed, or if another puppy is imminent, remove the puppy to his warming box. A towel over the box will prevent heat loss. Once the puppy has nursed he will be quite happy to settle down to a nap in the interior of his warm box.

If the puppy will not nurse he may be too cold, especially if he is complaining but not doing anything. A good rub with a cloth or a warm-up in the box will usually set him right.

Sometimes a Bullmastiff will have her puppies every half hour, sometimes the intervals are longer. Do not let her go more than about two hours as a delay might indicate a problem and may cause the loss of others waiting in line. If this happens call your vet and discuss it with him or her.

You will have to watch the bitch carefully to tell when she has had her last puppy as Bullmastiffs can have anywhere from four to sixteen. She will normally tell you when she thinks she has finished by settling down for a well-earned sleep. Before she finally settles down, make sure she goes outside and relieves herself. She must do this to ensure her bladder is functioning properly. Most owners need to be a little firm to get the mother to go outside as the last thing she wants to do is leave her brood.

Most whelpings seem to happen at night. If this is the case for your bitch, take her out the following morning and walk her until she evacuates her bowels. Although stimulating milk supply, consumption of the afterbirths also causes constipation. It is advisable not to allow her to eat more than one or two if possible but sometimes it can be difficult to intervene at the appropriate time. She must pass this to allow her bowels to function properly. It will normally appear as a malodorous black, tarry substance, but the sight of it means all is well.

If by chance your bitch has no milk you will have to hand feed the puppies until they are able to feed themselves at about three weeks. In this

Weaning can be a pleasant, but messy, activity.

Tailwynde's Nine One One (Photo courtesy A. Pfenniger)

case check with your breeder what formula you should use, how much and how often. After feeding you will have to play mother and rub the puppy's stomach and genital area with a wet face cloth to imitate the action of a mother's tongue and cause the puppy to relieve itself. Sometimes a milkless bitch will oblige and do the licking for you, but it is better to be prepared. Keep a daily check on the puppies' weights as a guide to see if they are getting enough food.

Problems during whelping

Most whelpings go very easily but now and again there are certain warning signs that things are not going quite as they should. It is best to be ready for these moments so you are not taken unawares.

The best solution to this is to ask your breeder for help and advice. The years of experience of your breeder can save you a lot of grief, so ask, and listen.

Weaning to Eight Weeks

When the puppies reach the age of three weeks, the bitch will start to object to their new teeth. Up until this time she will have taken care of all toilet cleaning, licking it up as if it were ambrosia. Remember

C.I.B. & Fi & Se & Ru & Lt Ch & LtW-10 Bullgrin's Hold The Tiger
Photo Credit: Riikka Holappa

that when weaning time comes you have to be mother, so save large quantities of newspaper and prepare for cleaning up chores.

At about the age of three weeks you will notice a decided lack of enthusiasm on the part of the bitch to stay with her pups for any length of time because of their teeth. Bullmastiff puppies seem to grow teeth like vampires once they start. The puppies may want milk but the last thing the bitch wants is to have a bunch of very active puppies leaping at her and grabbing a mouthful of nipple with sharp teeth. Besides the discomfort, the constant grabbing can damage her mammaries and cause bleeding, infection and permanent damage.

To avoid this, you should watch carefully for the first signs so you can start the weaning process. Puppies will always prefer to lie there sucking effortlessly than to have to work for their food by competing for it or exerting any effort. At 17–21 days the puppies should begin trying to get up and run about. Occasionally there will be a lazy pup who prefers to lie there like a blimp, especially if the mother is a good nurser. Another reason for inactivity is that the puppies' feet might be slipping on the floor. If a puppy has tried repeatedly to stand up and run only to slip back into place, he will lie there and nurse without any further attempt. The problem with this attitude is the puppy's weight is increasing; if it increases while the puppy remains in the lying position the front legs are pushed wider and wider apart. Eventually this 'swimmer' is too heavy for the weak muscles to lift him up and this

Can Ch Shayla's Vigilante O' Banbury (Photo courtesy L.& P. Rehsler)

becomes a permanent feature. Therefore, make sure a non-slip surface is provided. If the puppy still proves to be lazy, remove the bitch from the whelping box for a long enough time to make the puppy very hungry. It is amazing to see an apparently helpless puppy struggle up and walk when mother is close by and the pup is hungry. This kind of puppy must obviously be trimmed down in weight and a little hunger will soon attend to the matter.

A puppy will ignore a bowl of softened food for the readily-available milk supply lying close by. The secret to weaning is competition. Take the puppy food of choice and dilute it to make a sloppy, watery mixture. It is wise to dilute the puppy version of the dog food you intend to use when the puppies get old enough for solid food. Do not add sundry items to this mixture as you will only cause stomach upsets. Do not use any cow's milk. The lacto bacillus bacteria in the puppy is the same as that in the bitch's milk, so if you introduce another you have a likely candidate for diarrhoea. If your puppy has a digestive problem, the naturally homogenised milk from a female goat is easily digestible and readily acceptable.

After the last feed take your bitch away and let her enjoy her day well away from the pups. When feeding time comes again the puppies will start to complain and you must be sure to prevent the bitch's natural instinct to answer this call. When another half hour has gone by, introduce your puppy bowl with your mixture. Hunger will drive the puppies to investigate a possible source of nourishment and most take quite naturally to lapping, sucking, or slipping their way through the gooey mix. Most end up wearing some of it.

When they have had enough, and this is quite soon the first time, let the mother go into the whelping box. She will be greeted by shrieks of welcome from the pups, but when they come to nurse they quickly find their appetite has diminished. Mother will do a nice clean-up of heads and tails and the puppies will sleep well that night with a good solid meal in their stomachs. Start weaning feeds at four-hour intervals and adjust this as the meals get heavier.

The mixture can become more solid at each subsequent mealtime. If at one meal it seems a little too much work for the puppies, return to yesterday's mix and try again tomorrow. The reduction in suckling will help the bitch's milk supply to dry up gradually. Once the pups are eating well in this manner the bitch can be moved to her own quarters to allow her peace and quiet.

There is an age-old remedy for drying up the bitch's milk after weaning which still works well. For about three or four days, reduce the bitch's water intake (but not enough to cause dehydration). Smooth camphor oil onto the mammaries in the morning and vinegar in the evening, and you will find the bitch regains her girlish figure very quickly without the characteristic droop associated with matrons. Do not rub

Aus Ch Bullmaster US Marshall (Photo: J. Karina)

quickly without the characteristic droop associated with matrons. Do not rub these mixtures onto her, as the rubbing will stimulate milk production. Once you have started this procedure, do not allow the puppies to nurse as the camphor is harmful to them.

Your bitch may have been a good mother, but very likely wants her own space back as soon as her puppies have left home. Therefore she may not enjoy the company of any of her pups after weaning. The Bullmastiff owner will have to watch for this and take care that the bitch's natural territorial attitudes do not create problems in the household. A word of caution to novice breeders: take care if you reintroduce puppies to the bitch after a separation. Some mothers are loving and only too pleased to see their young. However, many have no time for this reunion, having resumed their prior role as protector and territorial patrol dog. If this is the case the bitch may not welcome the intrusion of 'strange' dogs on her ground, even if they are her young. Such territorial behaviour must be carefully watched to avoid any trouble. If the bitch shows an obvious antipathy, take the puppies well away; do not risk trouble. It is a wonderful sight to see a bitch playing with her weaned young, but the converse is not so good. Different cultures have varied ideas but most agree that the best time to worm puppies is at three, six and nine weeks of age. It makes no sense to feed good food to nematodes.

Before this time has arrived you should have had a discussion with your vet concerning vaccination of the litter. The vaccination will again depend on the situation relating to the most feared diseases of distemper, hepatitis, leptospirosis, parvovirus, and corona. These are not words meant to scare you, but real potential epidemics if you do not attend to them. Most breeders and vets agree that these vaccinations must all be taken care of by no later than eight weeks. Further vaccinations will be advised at this time by your vet. In countries where rabies is a problem a vaccination will be given after the puppies are three months old.

CHAPTER EIGHT

Bullmastiff Breed Standard

What is a Standard?

All pure-bred dogs started out as cross-breeds from whatever strains were indigenous to them, evolving in accordance with local circumstances. Eventually the people would rely on the dogs to do certain jobs for them and fulfil a particular criterion. In some cases it was guarding the flocks; in some, herding sheep; in others a tracking nose, or the ability to go to ground after vermin, led to the dogs being used for these purposes.

All the early dogs were used for one or more specific functions, as they could not be kept for amusement or play; they had to earn their living. Ultimately the dog owners would agree on what was needed to satisfy their requirements for a dog to do some specific job. In most cases the choices of type were entirely dependent on function, with no aesthetic considerations whatsoever. Even the white coat of the Sealyham terrier was a functional one so that Captain Edwards, the breed originator, would not mistake his dog for a fox and shoot it by mistake. Once the physical type had been agreed the owners of the breed worked together to perfect the functional and physical characteristics of their dogs. When kennel clubs appeared on the scene it was to these 'fanciers' of common intent and agreement that the kennel clubs looked for guidance in determining the standards needed for the breed in question. To this day, breed standards are determined in the same way.

The autonomous kennel club of every country has the right to re-determine the criteria for any breed. This would happen, for instance, if the standard set down by the breed's country of origin did not use the same terminology as that current in the country of adoption, and ignored local factors governing the development of the breed. Many countries prefer to use the standard of the country of origin as a guide, modifying it later as the breed interest intensifies.

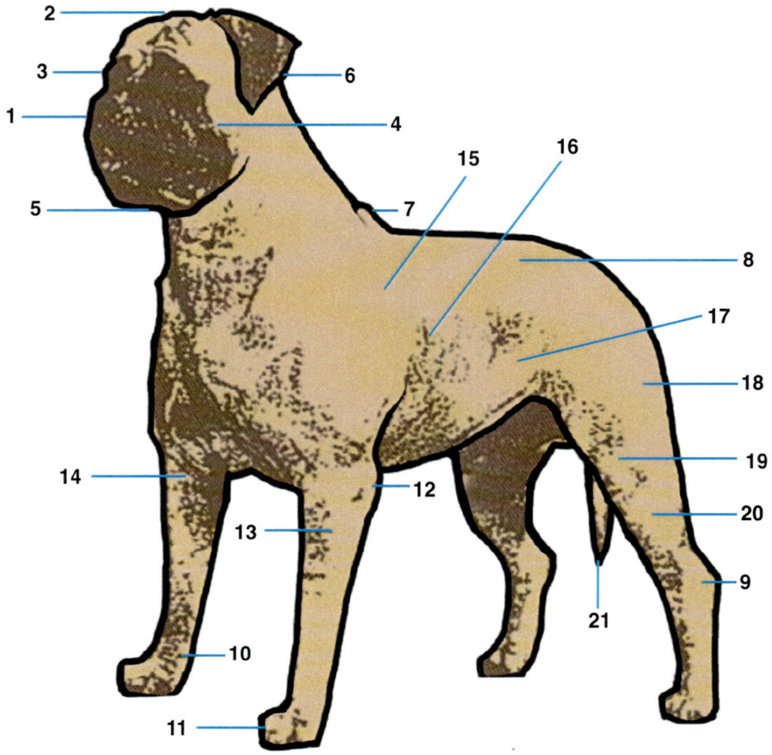

The parts of the Bullmastiff.

1. Muzzle
2. Occiput
3. Stop
4. Cheek
5. Flew
6. Arch of neck
7. Withers
8. Loin
9. Hock
10. Pastern
11. Toes
12. Point of elbow
13. Forearm (humerus)
14. Brisket
15. Shoulder
16. Ribs
17. Flank
18. First thigh
19. Stifle
20. Second thigh
21. Tail

The Bullmastiff

Many hours can be spent discussing each country's development of the breed since its acceptance in Great Britain by the Kennel Club in 1924. In all too many countries where similar dogs have been separated by time and distance a parochial development has evolved based on local ideas

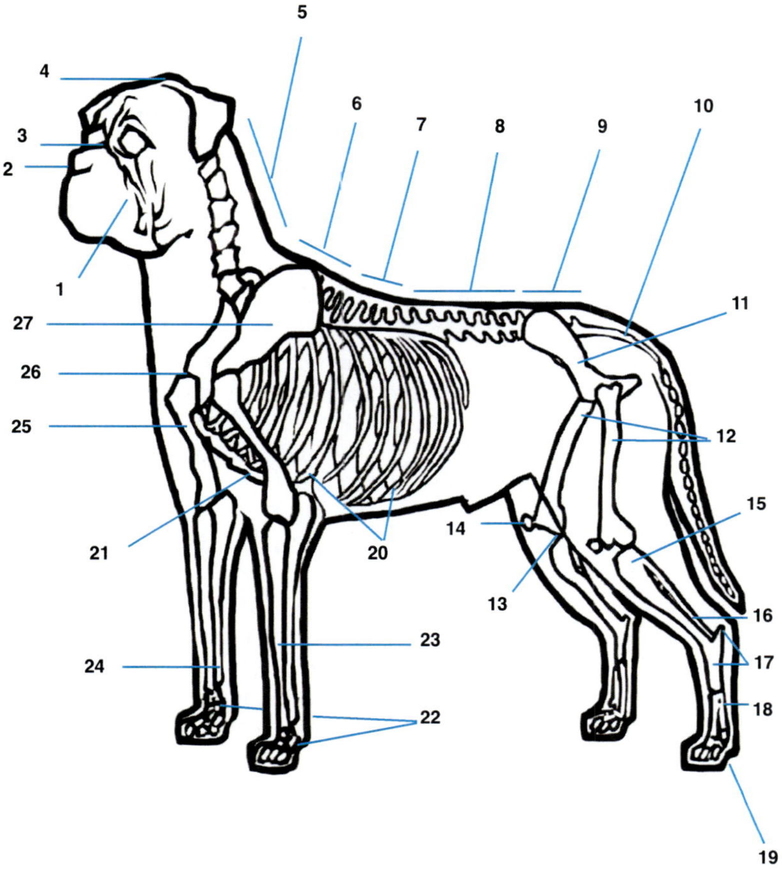

Anatomy of the Bullmastiff.

1 Cheek
2 Nose
3 Stop
4 Occiput
5 7 cervical vertebrae– Neck
6 8 Dorsal vertebrae– Withers
7 5 dorsal vertebrae – Back
8 7 lumbar vertebrae – Loin
9 3 sacral vertebrae–Croup
10 3–26 vertebrae– Tail
11 Pelvic bone – hip
12 Femur or upper thigh
13 Stifle or knee joint
14 Patella or knee cap
15 Tibia
16 Fibula
17 Hock joint or heel
18 Hock or metatarsals
19 Toes or phalanges
20 Ribs (13 pairs)
21 Sternum or breastbone
22 Pastern or metacarpals
23 Ulna
24 Radius
25 Humerus – upper foreleg
26 Shoulder joint
27 Scapula or shoulder blade

and nationalistic pride, formulating a separate breed.

One of the amazing things is the continuity that has followed the Bullmastiff in most of its adoptive countries. To simplify the explanation, understand that Britain, the originator of the breed, recently revised its Standard very slightly from one that had been in use for many, many years. Upon examination it will be seen that Australia's Standard is a virtual carbon copy of the revised standard, while New Zealand's is a carbon copy of the original British Standard.

South Africa uses the original British Standard as its base with a few changes in terminology but not in meaning, probably for easier regional understanding. An admirable addition to the end of the South African Standard is the space given to comments on personality traits, the adult dog, and temperament. This is a far-sighted addition which can only assist novice owners and should be considered by other countries.

Although the thought of an International Standard on Bullmastiffs creates logistical nightmares, it is interesting that the commonwealth countries mentioned are attempting just that within their jurisdictions. This approach at least attempts to bring the type into common line and allows the avenues of modern communication to remove physical distance barriers.

Another member of the commonwealth, Canada, seems to have taken the task of type control one step further. Canada is a country of merging ethnic backgrounds, many of them non-commonwealth, who may not know or care about Bullmastiffs. Perhaps this is why the Canadian Standard has gone to great lengths to ensure a future understanding of the Bullmastiff Standard by extraneous specific descriptions. To avoid confusion in contemplating all of the standards, similar enough to be one giant standard (with regional differences) it is the Canadian Standard that is used in this book to keep things simple. For the minor differences of your standard, take a few minutes to check if you are not sure. Old time British exhibitor/breeder and breed judge Mr H J Price makes the following comments on the Breed Standard:

"In my opinion the standard for any breed of dog should be that of its country of origin. What use is there in importing a dog and then changing its looks or type? To me this seems a pointless exercise.

Basically there is no difference between any of the standards. Therefore we have a universally accepted Bullmastiff that can be exhibited and win in any country, which is as it should be.

Our standard has stood for many years with only minor additions or alterations. It is not complicated, but easily understood by all. That it has stood for so long is a tribute to those who wrote the original standard. Over the years there have been those who sought to make changes; mostly I would suggest those who wanted to make the standard fit their dogs and always those who had very little knowledge of the breed.

The Bullmastiff is now recognised world-wide. I would not suggest that everyone follows our standard; far from it! But I would say let us keep at least a similar basically acceptable standard."

As a show judge, I totally agree with Mr Price on this, and it should be applied to all breeds.

Why Is a Bullmastiff the Way He Is?

The criteria for the Bullmastiff did not happen by accident. There was definite reasoning behind the decisions of the early gamekeepers to 'design' the Bullmastiff the way he was. The gamekeeper was using an animal against men who had nothing to lose but their lives and everything to gain by fighting back. The gamekeepers had to produce a dog that could withstand any and all abuse that these desperate, intelligent poachers could produce and all the dog had to defend himself with was his 'natural' physical body. Some of the points are obvious, others more subtle.

Head and skull

The skull is built like a square fortified box that allows for much punishment without the loss of all senses. If the dog is damaged on one side of the head the wideness and squareness allows for the dog still to function with the other side. A narrow or snipey skull could easily be crushed by a foot or club but the wide broad skull prevents this. The eyes at each side of the wide head act as the same safeguard. If one eye is damaged the other side of the head can still work and if the dog is hit squarely across the face the flatness can take the blow whereas a Borzoi-type dog would be killed.

The muzzle performs in parallel to the head. The wideness and 'chopped-off' appearance assures minimum damage and allows the dog the greatest leverage if he has to grab the intruder's club or stick. The wide-spaced canines and flat-fronted muzzle permit the dog to hold very tightly with his strong cheek muscles and yet continue to breathe. The abbreviation of flews ensures a relatively dry mouth that will not slide or slip while the dog is gripping.

The ears are small to prevent the poacher or intruder from gaining an advantage by grabbing the dog's ears and using the hand hold as a means to free himself from the dog.

Light eyes have always been a fault in this breed. If you are lying in wait for an intruder the last thing you need is for him to see the moon reflecting off your dog's eyes. The dark eyes form an integral part of the mask effect to break up the outline of the dog's face in the dark. Light eyes would show up well against the dark marking that surrounds Bullmastiff's eyes

.

Forequarters

A Bullmastiff is not a dog that pursues its prey and jumps on it as a German Shepherd might. The Bull mastiff is a 'knock down and pin' dog. To do

[Please read this section carefully! What you don't want to see as a Judge or an Exhibitor, is a poorly masked dog with huge pendulous flews and long ears!! This is now too common and ignored for the sake of diplomacy. The breed is not being helped by this action and dogs exhibiting this scenario should be penalized accordingly

When reference is made to the square head, this is just what it means SQUARE, like a cube. The muzzle should also be a cube. This dog is built like this to take all the human abuse a poacher can throw at it - kicking, gouging, striking with a cudgel etc., so there is reason for these requirements in the breed. Long flews and long ears make superb handles for someone to repel the dog in a fight - usually meaning the dog will get hurt - listen to the reasoning of the old Gamekeepers who wanted to keep their dogs and themselves alive!

1. Muzzle should be square at end and chopped off - not triangular as often seen today.

2. Flews should not be lower than the bottom jaw, and not hanging.

3. Check the incisors: dogs are now appearing with two different types of incisors - some Bulldog, some Mastiff.

Checck and compare to your standaard

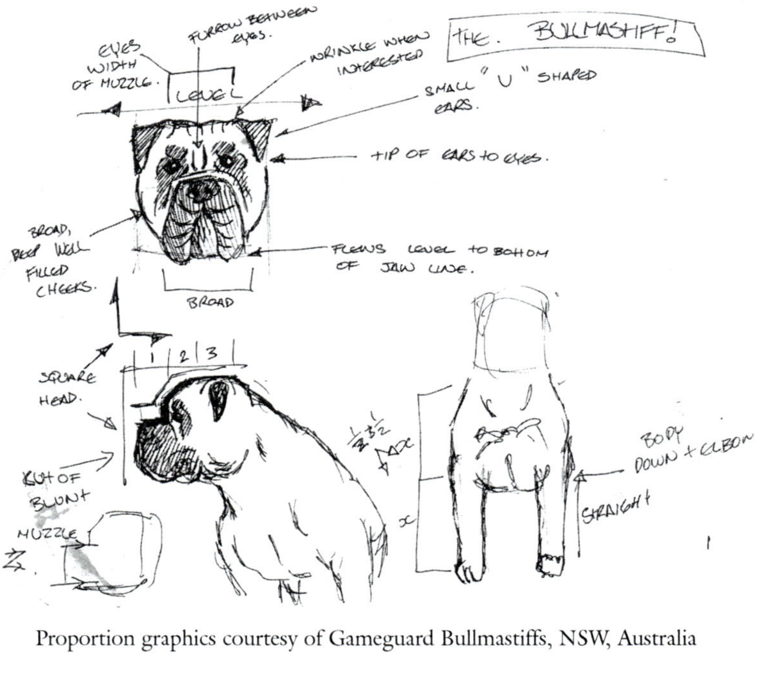

Proportion graphics courtesy of Gameguard Bullmastiffs, NSW, Australia

Proportion graphics courtesy of
Gameguard Bullmastiffs,
NSW, Australia

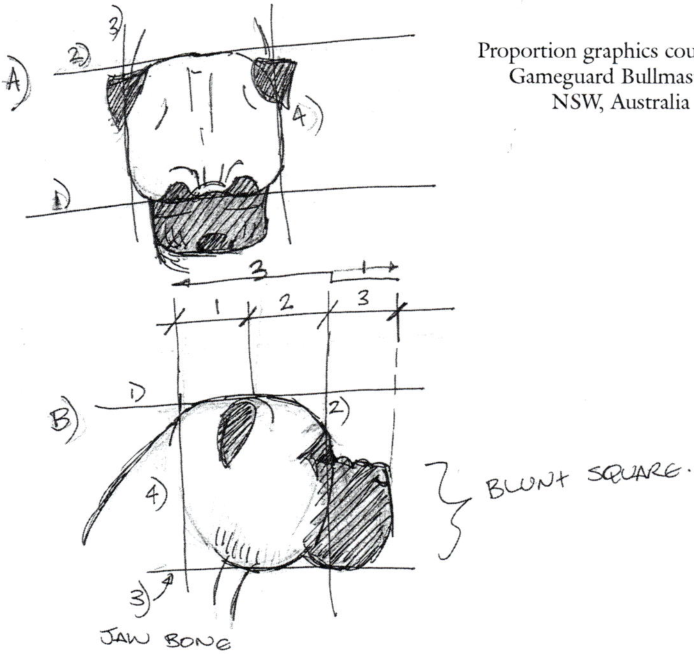

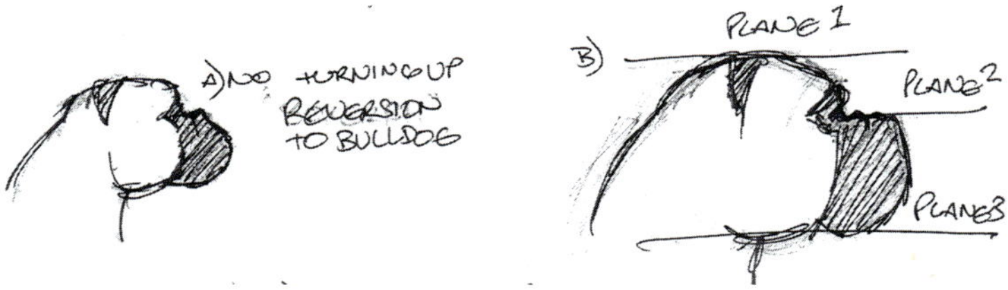

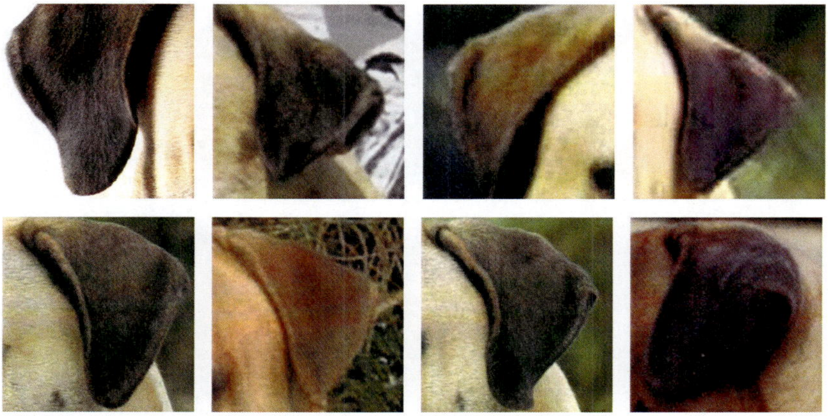

Ears of well known Bullmastiffs - Check the standard, what do you think?

the knocking down the Bullmastiff uses its huge chest of great width and depth as a bulldozer would use its blade. To achieve this the Bullmastiff needs its chest and the accompanying wide stance and shoulder muscles.

The correct proportion of his upper and lower front legs give the proper leverage and balance as the dog hits the intruder.

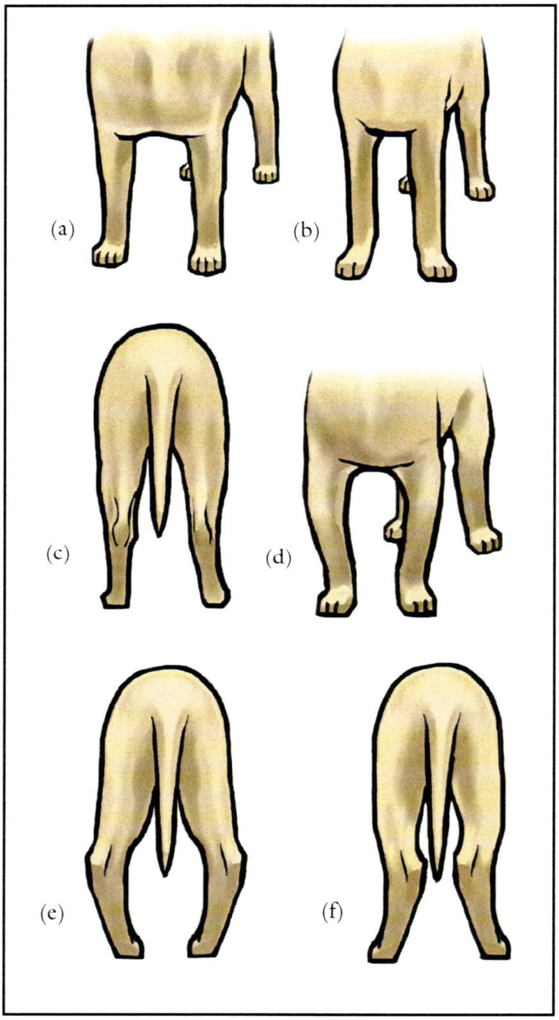

(a) Good forequarters. (b) Poor forequarters (narrow front). (c)Good hindquarters. (d) Out at elbow. (e) Sickle hocked. (f) Cow hocked.

(a)

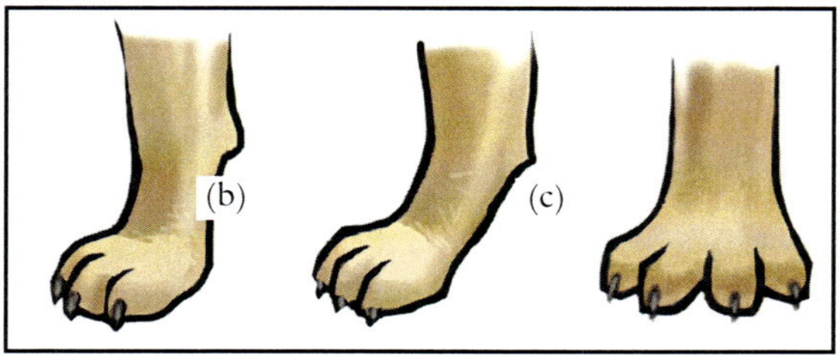

The feet. (a) Good pastern. (b) Slack pastern. (c) Splay foot.

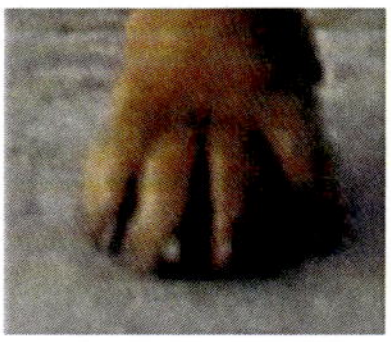

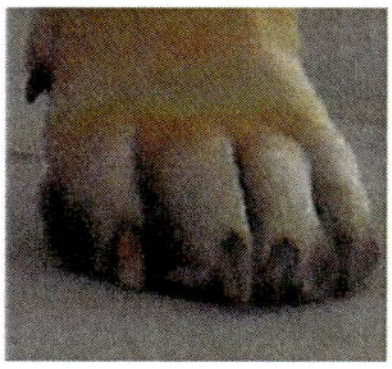

[Dogs with shortened upper arms will exhibit short necks set in verloaded shoulders and usually no arch at all - just stuck on
One of the attributes of the Gamekeeper's dog was the ability to knock a poacher to the ground with its chest - rather like a battering ram. The pro sternum associated with a correct shoulder could do this well. In recent years, the reasoning behind this has been lost. Many dogs today are walking around with shortened upper arms as a result of incorrect breeding.
cont'd next page

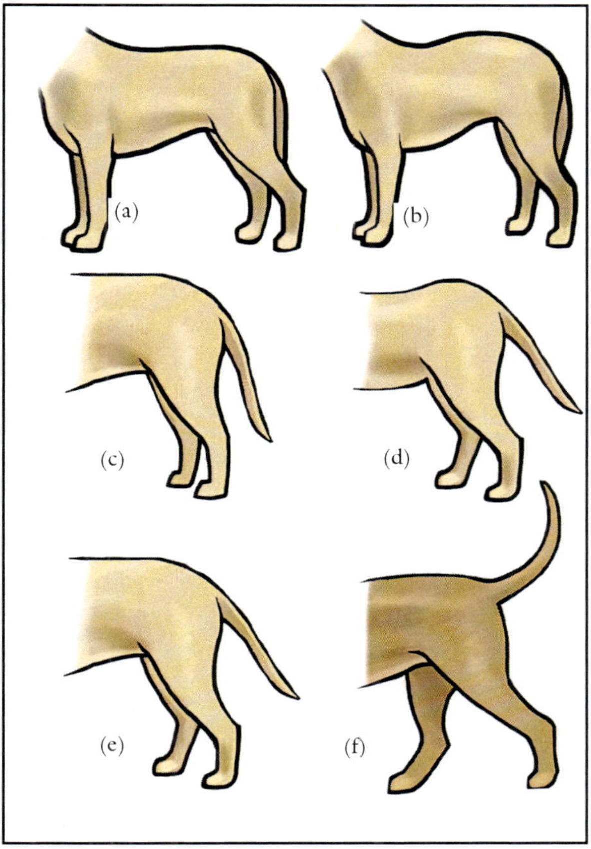

(a) Well balanced. (b) Roach backed. (c) Straight stifle.
(d) Sway backed. (e) Good tail carriage.
(f) Hound or gay tail.

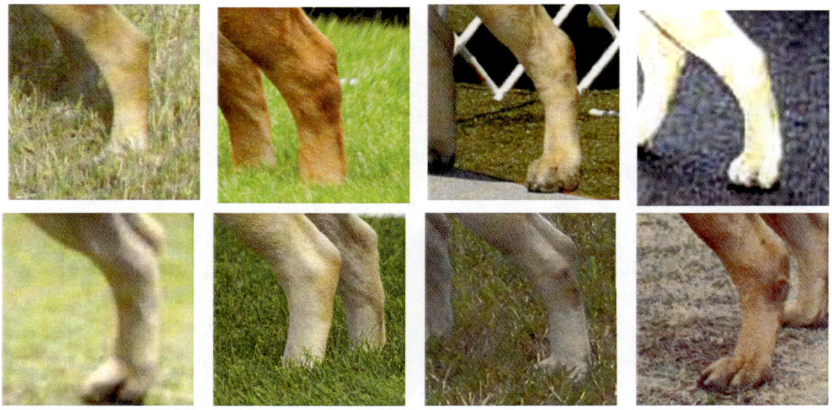

Hocks of well-known dogs .. Check your standard, what to you think?

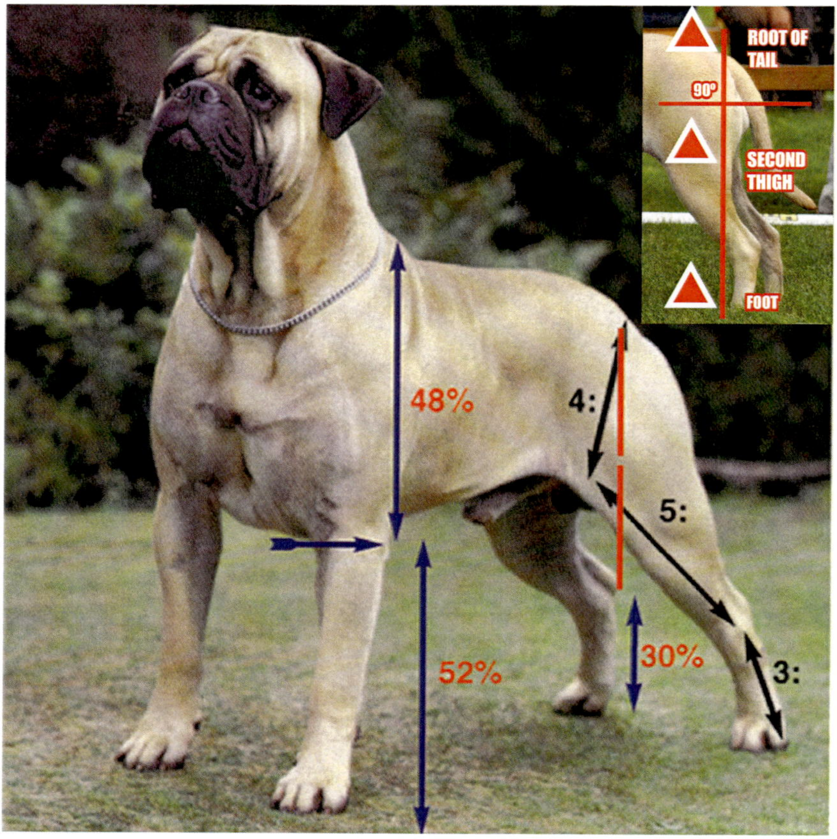

This shortening of the upper arm results in the angle of the shoulder becoming less and less until the tip of the shoulder blade (scapula) is above the level of the spine resulting in an overloaded shoulder, shortness of reach and straightening of the front (see diagram xx). It is essential to work towards the optimum shoulder angles and ignore the trends of uninformed breeders who breed for looks and forget the form and function.] In a good rear end, root of tail, second thigh, and toe are all in same vertical plane (see diagram). Author's comment

Back and hindquarters

The forequarters and hindquarters work together as one. The hind end supplies the power to move the dog from his lying position to an immediate charging mode, delivering power and speed to the business front end to knock down the adversary. All this is delivered through the connecting transmission of the dog's back. To coordinate the front and rear into an efficient working team the dog needs a powerful short back that will not suffer from weakness of length or rigidity of shortness, giving the dog the ability to twist and turn. Hindquarters should have well-developed second thighs to allow quick action from a lying position.

Feet

The feet are described as arched, well-muscled, cat-like. The dog was not operating in wide open spaces, but rather in and out of thickets and trees. To do this well the dog needed strong feet that could pivot his weight and bulk around trees and up rock faces; in the most adverse surface areas, he also needed strong, hard pads.

Tail

Many people think of a tail as an unnecessary extra piece at the back end of the dog. The Bullmastiff needed his tail as a counterbalance as he did his twisting and turning. A dog's body works like a cantilever bridge and must always be kept in balance. The work of a Bullmastiff emphasises this perfectly.

Coat

In his original role, the Bullmastiff must have spent many wet and uncomfortable hours lying in the grass waiting for his quarry. It is obvious that he would need a weatherproof coat to do this job; otherwise he would not have lasted long. Originally, gamekeepers favoured brindle for their dogs. A good brindle has a base colour (usually of fawn or red) with vertical tiger striping. Quite often today unknowing fanciers will refer to any dark colouring on a lighter background as brindle, but this is not true. The striping of a brindle was as valuable to the early gamekeeper and his night dog as stripes are for a zebra's survival on the savanna of Africa. The Bullmastiff had to blend in with the background to give him and his master every advantage.

BULLMASTIFF STANDARD (CANADIAN)

Note:

Faults are classified as Serious or Minor, indicated as (S) and (M) respectively. Note that minor faults are points which would not of themselves contribute to unsoundness in the dog, or are the result of poor conditioning, which might be controlled, and are not likely to be hereditary.

Origin and purpose:

The Bullmastiff was developed in England by gamekeepers for protection against poachers. The foundation breeding of the modern pure-bred was 60% Mastiff and 40% Bulldog. It is a guard and companion dog, and should be loyal, obedient and thus suitable for training.

General appearance:

The Bullmastiff is a powerfully built, symmetrical dog, showing great strength and activity, but not cumbersome; upstanding and compact in appearance, with breadth and depth of skull and body, the latter set on strong, sturdy, well boned legs. The height measured vertically from the ground to the highest point of the withers, should nearly equal the length measured horizontally from the forechest to the rear part of the upper thigh, and should slightly exceed the height at the hips. Bitches are feminine in appearance, of somewhat lighter bone structure than the male, but should still convey strength. Faults: (S) Lack of balance. Poor or light bone structure. (M) Lack of muscular development. Ranginess.

Temperament:

The Bullmastiff should be bold, fearless and courageous, a dependable guard dog; alert and intelligent. Faults: (S) Viciousness. Shyness. (Such dogs should not be used for breeding.) (M) Apathy and sluggishness.

Size:

Height at the highest point of the withers – dogs, 25–27in; bitches, 24–26in. Weight: Dogs, 110–130lb; bitches, 100–120lb. It is important that weight be in proportion to height and bone structure, to ensure balance. Faults: (S) Over maximum height. Under minimum height. (M) Over maximum weight. Under minimum weight.

Coat and colour:

(a) Coat: short and dense, giving good weather protection. Faults: (S) Long, soft coat.(M) 'Staring' coat, which means poor condition. (b) Colour: Any shade of red, fawn or brindle, but the colour to be pure and clear. A small white marking on chest permissible but not desirable. Faults: (S) White markings other than on chest. (M) Black shading on body, legs or tail (of reds or fawns).

Head:

(a) Skull: The skull should be large, equal in breadth, length and depth, with a fair amount of wrinkle when the dog is interested; well developed cheeks. The skull in circumference may measure the height of the dog. Forehead flat, with furrow between the eyes. Stop definite. Faults:(S) Narrow skull. Shallow skull. (M) Domed forehead. Insufficient stop. (b)

Muzzle:

The muzzle should be short, broad and deep, in the same proportion as the skull. The distance from the tip of the nose to the stop should not exceed one-third of the length from the tip of the nose to the centre of the occiput. Broad under the eyes and nearly parallel in width to the

Fin Se Uch Maxinice Jolie Roug - Photo credit: Tiina Orava

end of the nose; blunt and cut off square, appearing in profile in a plane parallel to the line of the skull. A black mask is essential. The nose should be black; flat; broad with widely spreading nostrils when viewed from the front.Flews not too pendulous. The lower jaw broad. Faults: (S) Muzzle too long, too narrow, pointed or lacking in depth. Muzzle too short; nostrils set on top; nose pointed, upturned or laid back; lower jaw narrow. (M) Lack of wrinkle; flews too pendulous. Disqualifications: Liver mask. No Mask. (c) Teeth: Preferably level bite or slightly undershot. Canine teeth large and set wide apart; other teeth strong, even and well placed. Faults: (S) Teeth overshot. Teeth more than 0.25in undershot. Wry mouth. (M) Irregular or poorly placed teeth. Small teeth. (d) Eyes: Dark or hazel, and of medium size; set apart the width of the muzzle. Faults: (M) Light eyes. Eyes too close together, too large, too small. Disqualifications: Yellow eyes. (e)

Ears:

V-shaped and carried close to the cheeks; set on wide and high, level with the occiput, giving a square appearance to the skull which is important. They should be darker in colour than the body, and the point of the ear, when alert, should be level with the eye. Faults: (S) Rose ears. (M) Ears too long or too short. Lack of darker colour.

Neck:

Well arched, of moderate length, very muscular, and almost equal in circumference to the skull. Faults: (S) Neck too short; too long. Neck weak and scrawny.

Forequarters:

Proper angulation and proportionate bone lengths of the forequarters are very important. The shoulder bone should slope forward and downward from the withers at an angle of 45 degrees from the vertical. The humerus (upper arm) should form a right angle with the shoulder bone, 45 degrees from the vertical. The shoulder bone and humerus should be approximately equal in length. The length of the foreleg from the ground to the elbow should be a little more than half the distance from the ground to the withers, approximately 52%. The shoulders and upper arms should be muscular and powerful, but not overloaded. Forelegs powerful, with round heavy bone, vertical and parallel to each other, set well apart; elbows set close to the body. Pasterns straight and strong. Feet of medium size, not turning in or out, with round toes, well arched. Pads thick and tough. Nails black. Faults: (S) Lack of proportion in bone. Shoulders too steep. Shoulders overloaded. Elbows turned in or out. Lack of bone in forelegs. Forelegs bowed. Weak pasterns. Splay feet. (M) Feet turned in or out. White nails.

Body and tail:

(a) Body: Compact. Chest wide and deep, with ribs well sprung and well set down between the forelegs. Back short and level. Loins wide, muscular; croup slightly arched, with fair depth of flank. Faults: (S) Body too long. Shallow chest. Narrow chest. Lack of rib-spring. Sway back. Roach back. Tip of hip bone higher than withers. (M) Too much tuck-up. (b) Tail: Set on high, strong at the root and tapering to the hocks. It may be carried straight or curved. Faults: (S) Screw tail. Crank tail. Tail set too low. (M) Tail carried hound fashion. Too Long. Too short. Too heavily coated.

Hindquarters:

It is important that structure, angulation and proportionate bone lengths of the hindquarters be in balance with the forequarters. The pelvis (hip bone) should slope backward and downward from the spine at an angle of 30 degrees. The femur (upper thigh bone) should form a right angle with the pelvis. The lower thigh bone (stifle) should set an angle of 45 degrees to the vertical. The pelvis and femur should be approximately equal in length. The ratio of the lengths of the femur to the tibia-fibula, to the hock should be approximately as 4:5:3. The length of the lower leg, from the ground to the hock joint, should be a little less than 30% of the distance from the ground to the top of the hip bones. The lower leg should be vertical to the ground. The hips should be broad, in balance with shoulders and rib cage. Hind legs strong and muscular, with well developed second thighs, denoting power and activity, but not cumbersome, set parallel to each other and well apart, in balance with forelegs and body. Feet as in forequarters. Faults: (S) Lack of proportion in bone. Poor angulation at hip-bone. Narrow hip structure. Stifle too straight or over-angulated. Cow hocks. Bowed hind legs. Splay feet. (M) Feet turned in or out. White nails.

Gait:

The gait should be free, balanced and vigorous. When viewed from the side the dog should have good reach in the forequarters and good driving power in the hindquarters. The back should be level and firm, indicating good transmission from rear to front. When viewed from the front (coming toward) or from the rear (going away), at a moderate pace, the dog shall track in two parallel lines, neither too close together nor too far apart, so placed as to give a strong well-balanced movement. The toes (fore and hind) should point straight ahead.

Direction to exhibitors and judges:

The dog should be moved in the ring at a sufficient speed to show fluidity of movement, and not at a slow walk. Faults: (S) Rolling, paddling, or weaving when gaited. Any crossing movement, either front or rear. Stilted and restricted movement. (Dogs with structural weakness as evidenced by poor movement should not be used for breeding.)

Disqualifications:

Liver mask. No mask. Yellow eyes. (Note: this is a Canadian opinion, not shared by other standards - check yours).

[As the "Mask" problem has caused many challenges over the years. The "Mask" is the area of the foreface between the stop and the nose. So .... a black nose is not part of the mask. Always remember that the purpose of the mask was to create a break in the open face of the dog to assist it in not being seen by the poacher in lowlight or darkness. So, in effect, the mask is a camouflage effect in the dog's face. Not so important in the brindle dogs, whose muzzles were black anyway, but definitely necessary for the fawn and some red dogs. - See your standard's glossary.

CHAPTER NINE
The Problem Times

Flying Ears

ike all young animals, your puppy will have a certain amount of stress when he starts to teethe. One of the many ways he shows this is by drooling like a human baby. It is an unpleasant time for your young puppy; his baby teeth are falling out, his mouth is tender, and anything he bites to take away this feeling makes the pain worse. This is the time when your puppy's mature teeth are erupting and, judging by the size of the incoming teeth, it is anything but a pleasant experience.

Depending on the pedigree line, most teething is over by the fourth month, although it does sometimes carry on a little further. One of the tell-tale signs of teething problems is the development of your puppy's ears.

During the time of actual teething, the stress causes the puppy to 'rose' his ears. This is when the ears are pulled back against the side of the head. In extreme cases the burr of the ear is seen.

In most cases the ears return to their natural position against the cheek once teething is over. However, if the teething is particularly bad or the dog has small ears they may have pulled back so far that the muscles do not return the ears to their normal position.

At about five months the cartilage in the ears starts to harden. This means that if your puppy's ears are still rosed at this time they will stay in that position permanently. If the ears show no sign of settling down at about four-and-a-half months it is wise to consider taping them with heating duct tape. This is a simple remedy to bring your dog's ears back to normal, and it is completely painless, harmless and takes only a few days. Sounds simple and cheap? It is.

Take two pieces of heating duct tape about 15cm (6in) long and tear them both lengthwise down the middle, making four pieces in all. Next take another piece of duct tape about 8cm (3in) and tear it lengthwise down the middle as well, making two pieces. You should now have six pieces of tape, four 15cm pieces, and two 8cm pieces.

Ask someone to hold the head of the dog while you put the tape in place. Pull one of the ears out straight from the head and lay the first long piece on the inside of the top of the leather of the ear from the head outward. If the pieces are torn to the correct length there should be an excess of tape over the end of the ear by about 5cm (2in); this will form a tab. Next, lay another of the long pieces on the outside of the same ear leather in the same way as the first so that the two sticky edges of the tape connect on the top side of the ear leather at the tab end. Repeat the same procedure with the other ear and you will end up with a puppy who looks as if he has a strap hanging from each ear. It is important that the pieces of tape for each ear are put on in two steps. Do not try to put one piece on and fold it over. Although this may seem the smarter move, if you do this you risk rolling the leading edge of the ear, which you will not realise until you take the tapes off. .

When you have the two tabs in place pull the end of each tab under the chin of the dog quite tightly and use one of the 8cm (3in) pieces of tape to connect the two tabs. Attach the first piece so that the dry side is against the dog and the sticky side out. Use the second piece to cover the sticky exposed side of the tape under the chin to prevent it sticking to everything the puppy touches.

That is all there is to it. In most cases the connection under the chin can be cut after about three days and the ears will magically stay in place in a beautiful ear set. If the set is not quite right simply leaving the tabs on will create enough weight to pull the ears in place over the next few days. Whatever happens, do not leave the tape on for more than a week.

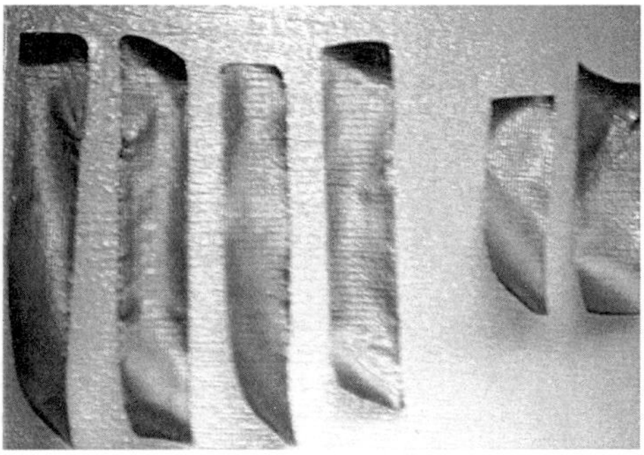

Above left: if the ear cartilage is allowed to harden in this position, the ear set will be spoiled.Above right: the four long and two short pieces of duct tape needed for ear correction.

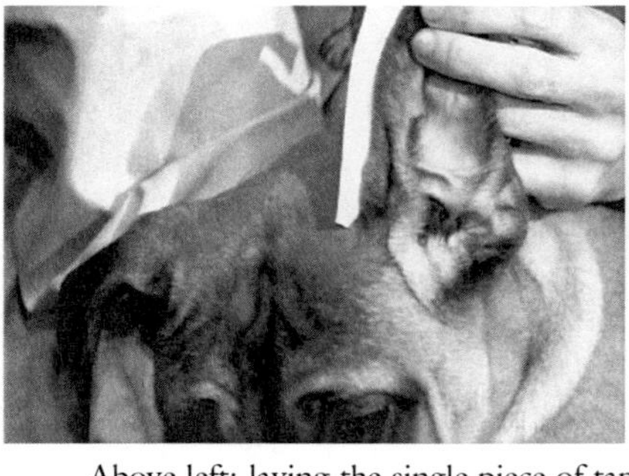

Above left: laying the single piece of tape on the outer edge of the ear leather. Above right: both ears taped with tab ends hanging prior to pulling ears in line.

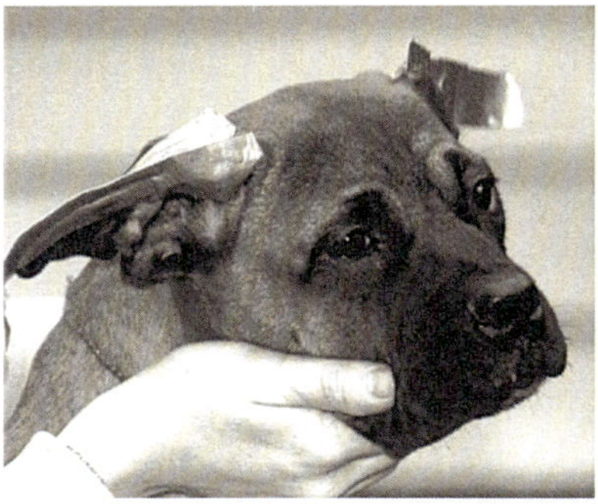

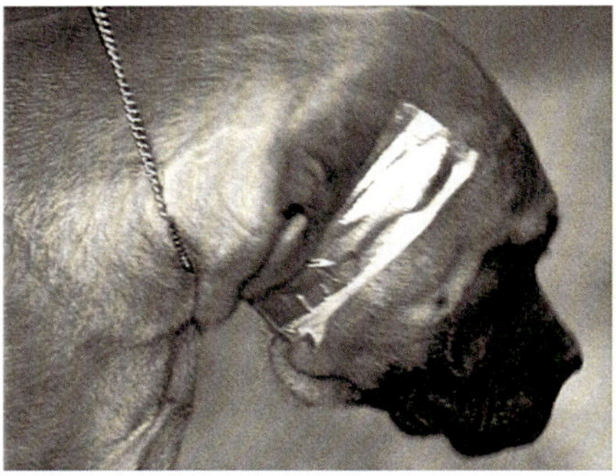

Above: ears pulled in tightly to head by joining the tabs under the chin. Ears seem to be pulled too tightly but this is necessary because of the elasticity of the area.

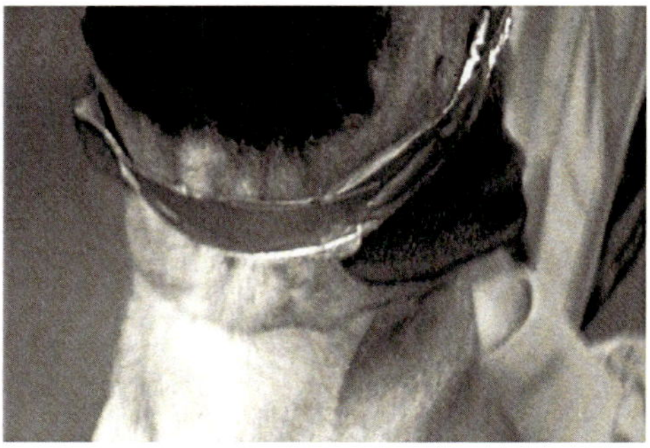

Above: the joining neck tab showing alignment of tape and ear edges pulled in straight line.

If you do this you risk causing ear infection as the ears are held close to the head for too long and the normal circulation of cooling air around the ears is interrupted.

If you remove the tape completely and the ears are not quite what you want, you can always retape them, but remember: the closer to five months the pup gets, the less chance of correction. When you see your dog as a mature animal with a perfect ear set you will appreciate the day you taped his ears.

Margarine will remove any residual tape glue left on the ear hair easily. Be sure to rinse the area well afterwards to prevent any adverse reaction.

The finished product. Compare this with the first photograph on page 121.

No Ch Maxinice Obi Wan Kenobi - Photo Credit: Marvin Solberg

Bloat and Gastric Torsion

This very disturbing condition can arise suddenly in the Bullmastiff, often with frightening rapidity. Statistically it only happens to 13 dogs in 10,000 but it is always sensible to be aware of the symptoms in case it happens to your dog.

What is it?

The syndrome is called gastric dilation-torsion. It is a big name for a bloated stomach that twists. This problem seems to affect the larger, deep-chested dog breeds more frequently than others. Simple dilation or bloating can occur at any age but is more frequently seen in young puppies when they have eaten too much too quickly. Gastric torsion can occur at any age but is seen more in older dogs and in more males than females.

How is it caused?

The torsion is initiated by a downward movement of the stomach which, because of the mechanics of its structure, starts a rotation of the stomach either clockwise or anti-clockwise. The direction is not so important as the fact that the gastric distension of the stomach as it twists compresses important veins and arteries in and around the stomach which are needed to nourish the blood cells and keep the blood clear in that area. As the problem increases the stomach impedes the functioning of the heart and lungs and, indirectly, the kidneys. If the situation is not relieved quickly the blood cells will die and prime organs will be irreparably damaged, resulting in perforation, shock and death. This is not meant to alarm you but to illustrate the importance of recognising the potential fatality of this problem and dealing with it immediately.

Symptoms

The usual signs of this problem are restlessness, salivation, retching with no resulting vomit, and abdominal distension. The distended stomach will feel hard and unresponsive to the touch, rather like a drum skin. Such signs develop about three hours after eating and are quite often associated with exercise after feeding. Most dogs will show an outward attitude of depression but the stress of their condition tends to excite them rather than making them stay quiet. Respiration will be rapid, laboured and shallow, typical of shock, and mucous membranes will often show a prolonged refill time.

The distended, hard stomach and a dog who is excited, frightened and in shock are symptoms very hard to miss even to the uninitiated. This is not a condition to be treated lightly. If you see these symptoms call your vet

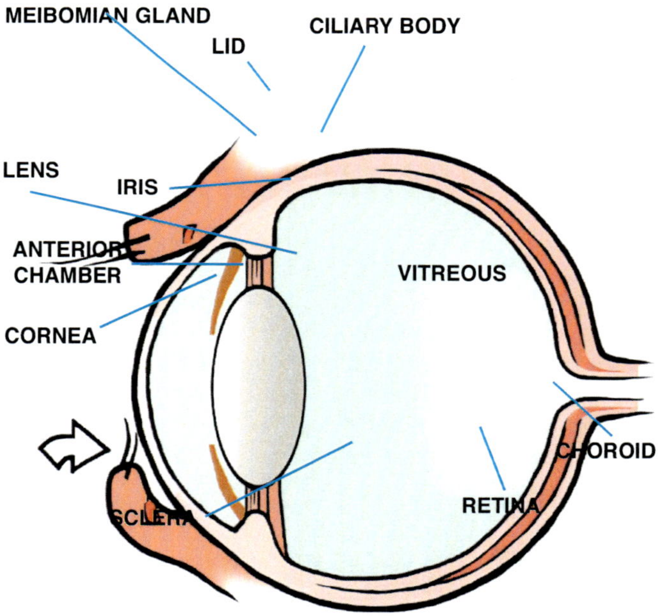

Entropion: the lower lid turns inwards, causing the eyelash to irritate the cornea (arrow indicates the problem).

immediately and don't take no for an answer! If your vet is away at the time go to your nearest emergency animal hospital. You will not get a second chance if it is gastric torsion; better a false alarm than a dead Bullmastiff.

Entropion

One of the things that always calls for comment from the all-knowing is the cause of runny eyes. In many cases it is nothing more than a draught that has caught the dog unawares and has resulted in a local irritation to the cornea of the eye, or the more common conjunctivitis. However, there is one more cause that occurs with more than its share of regularity and is never welcome or expected.

What is it?

The annoying problem is called entropion. Simply defined, this malady is described as the in-rolling of the eye lid and the accompanying eyelashes.

How is it caused?

It may be an acquired condition where the dog has run into a fence wire or caught his eye on a twig, but unfortunately it is all too often a congenital problem associated with certain pedigree lines.

Symptoms

Sometimes erroneously referred to as 'pink eye', entropion shows itself as discharge from the eye causing obvious irritation and annoyance to the dog. Careful examination will reveal the small hairs and eyelashes rubbing on the bulbous part of the eye. More often than not entropion affects only the lower lid but it can affect the upper as well. Neglect of this condition can lead to damage to the cornea of the eye, prolapse of the iris, and loss of the eye. Often the dog will avoid well-lit places and is seen to blink painfully. The hairs rubbing on the eye creates an ulceration of the eye's surface which often looks red and sore, hence the name of pink-eye.

Depending on the cause of the entropion, the solution may be an easy one. One action that should not be delayed is your call to your vet to determine which kind of entropion your Bullmastiff has and what should be done about it.

Osteochondritis Dissecans (OCD)

It is very normal and quite understandable that a young dog will be full of the joys of spring and want to romp around and jump up and down without a thought or care for what he is doing. One thing that nature does not supply young dogs with is common sense. It may seem fun to chase

THE SHORT UPPER ARM

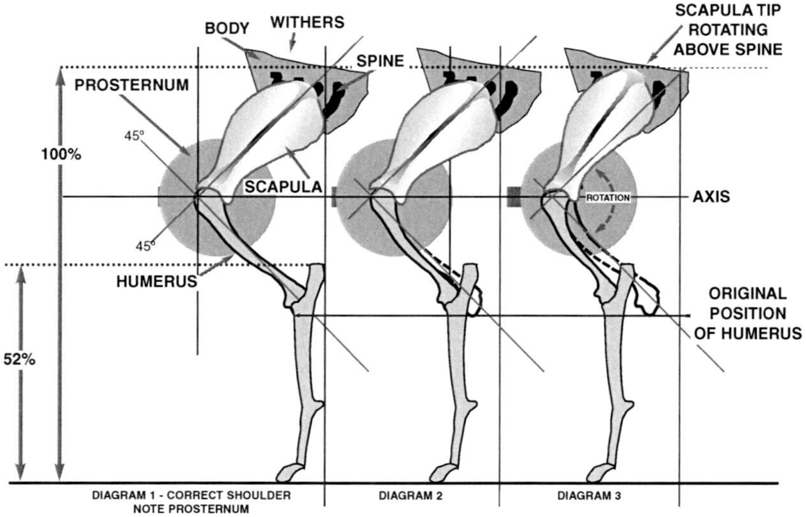

When the Bullmastiff comes towards me (as a Judge) it is sometimes painful to see this magnificent creature that, standing still, is every ounce a beautiful example of the breed, BUT coming towards me, instead of seeing an extended reach, driven by a driving rear, the dog is throwing its front legs around its rib cage as its upper arms are too short to handle the drive from behind, for it to extend its reach.

This has the effect of "rocking" the dog from side to side which is reflected in the slight sideways movement of the counter balancing head. Look carefully, the front legs don't come directly towards you, they come "around" the chest cavity, you can definitely see the dog throwing his "arms" around, not forward.

Diagram 1 is the type of shoulder and proportions we all want. Diagram 2 shows the effect of an upper arm that is, proportionately, shorter than it should be. Diagram 3 shows the extreme effect of a shorter upper arm In this case, not only has the dog a poor shoulder that gives the characteristic "rocking", but the edge of the scapula is now above the withers. As a Judge, when this happens the cartilage that compensates for this structure between the scapulae becomes rock hard so that the juncture between the two scapulae is absolutely solid! It makes it impossible to push the thumb down between the top of the scapulae. This dog now not only gives the rocking effect, and the throwing around of the upper arm, but the solidifying of the cartilage between the two scapulae giving the appearance of overloaded shoulders and restriction the already compromised front quarters. You will also notice the disappearance of the prosternum seen in a good shoulder structure.

the cat or young members of the household up and down the stairs, and most people would see nothing wrong with that. But what about jumping down from the back of a truck or a wall? Some people might think this quite normal and acceptable. Think, however, about all that weight coming down on the front legs and shoulders of a young Bullmastiff who still has a large amount of cartilage instead of bone. The mechanical force on the shoulders of, say, an eight-month-old is quite frightening. The result is that something has to give – and it will always be the cartilage, no matter how good the quality of life has been for the young dog.

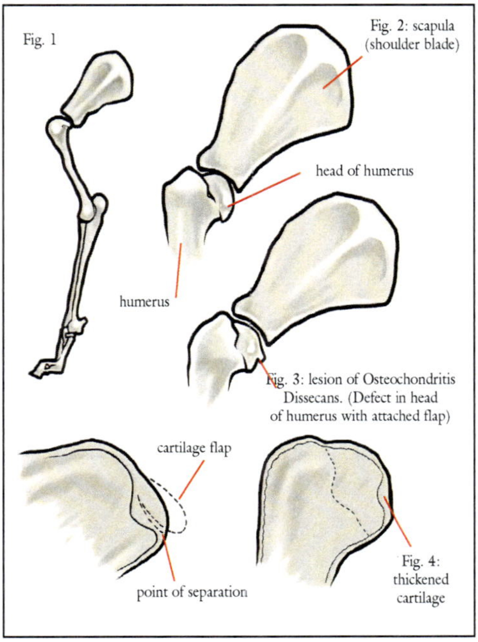

Osteochondritis Dissecans (OCD).

What is OCD?

In very basic terms, it is a chip of bone cartilage coming off the posterior (back) part of the head of the humerus (upper leg bone of front leg) which gets trapped between the socket joint of the shoulder and the ball of the head of the humerus.

How is it caused?

The head of the humerus is the 'ball' of the ball- and-socket joint of the shoulder (fig 1) which should be smooth and round (fig 2). In osteochondritis dissecans a section of the cartilage and underlying bone becomes partially or completely detached from the head of the humerus (fig 3). The flap of bone can float freely in the joint or may still retain a tenuous attachment to the head of the humerus. The consequence of this loose or detached chip in the joint is inflammation, arthritis and lameness.

Treatment

The treatment of this disease is, at best, controversial. Most authorities feel that if a large chip is present in the joint, especially if it is still attached, removal by surgery is the treatment of choice.

In mild cases (those with only a small defect in the head of the humerus and no flaps) some researchers suggest strict crate resting for several months and a recheck with X-rays to evaluate the problem area at a later date. If clinical lameness persists and/or the X-ray appearance worsens, surgery may still be performed.

Still other schools of thought have suggested that in some cases rigorous exercise will effect a cure by dislodging the flap from its attachment, causing it to be ground up and allowing the chip(s) to be absorbed and the defect in the humeral head to heal.

As in all such conditions, no consensus has yet been reached on the 'correct' method of treatment. Each vet will have a preference with which he is comfortable.

Hip Dysplasia (HD)

Hip dysplasia is a condition that affects the hip joints of dogs, usually dogs over 13kg (29lb) in weight. The equivalent in those less than 13kg (29lb) is called 'aseptic necrosis of the femoral joints'.

The dysplasia, or sub luxation as it is called by vets, occurs after the femoral head (ball joint) or the cavity (acetabulum) into which it fits in the pelvis has been modified to such an extent that the femoral head no longer fits correctly into the acetabulum, resulting in excessive movement of these two parts. The resultant distress that such movement causes to the joint can be well understood by the layman, as can the pain and arthritic condition that develops. Depending on the condition of the joints when HD is diagnosed, the relative severity can be assessed. In many cases, the pain is so severe and the dog so debilitated that the only kind and humane thing to consider is euthanasia. According to the medical profession, for many, many years HD has been considered a clear case of genetic inferiority of the parents of the dog carrying this dreadful condition.

What really shook the world of accepted HD data was Cornell University's evidence that HD was not 100% genetic but maybe only 25%, the remainder being environmental. What a shock! However, what did 'environmental' mean? Was that like genetic, only different? Most people accepted the word of Cornell but once again, how many asked, 'Why?' As with much research, principles change by modification every few years, so how accurate are these figures and will they change too? The previous certainty knocked down by this new one makes a breeder pause and wonder...

Collagen is the 'glue' that holds muscles together so if there is lots of good glue there are strong muscles, very little or no sub luxation and no acetabuli damage. X-rays are taken to diagnose HD but what they show us are the results of HD. The bone material and fibre may be fine under normal conditions but, if there is weak musculature that is not holding the ball joint in the acetabulum correctly, the ball joint of the femur will slide and move round until the acetabulum and ball joint are modified sufficiently enough to show up on an X-ray and result in a diagnosis of

HD. The apparent physical cause is determined as joint laxity, shallow acetabuli or joint ball head erosion but the observer may be looking at the symptom, not the cause. The use of sodium ascorbate could in itself account for the low rate of HD occurrences in Great Britain. Add to this the slower pace of life in Britain compared to North America and a totally less stressful way of life and a better environment emerges.

For many centuries the Masetheff, or mastiff type of dog, spent most of his day lolling around the manor house, stable or farm with no other concern than where the next meal was coming from. His life was mostly rural, low stress and self-fulfilling. His duties were often learned from an older, trained dog and by sympathetic induction he completed his life's chores. Compare this to today's dog. Higher intensity of social environment, close quarters with other animals, humans by the gross, noise, training, neurotic owners, vaccinations, surgery, showing... Just look at the trauma in a dog's eyes at the first show. The dogs, the noises, the public address system, irritated exhibitors, crowded quarters — a campaign trail where all these problems are compounded, plus the

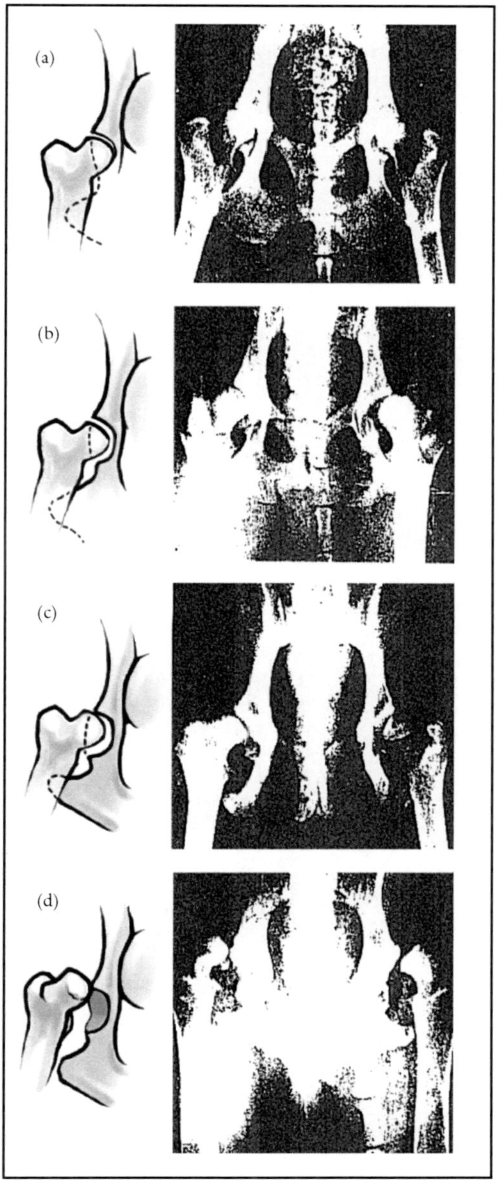

(a) This shows a normal hip joint with femoral head and socket in normal relationship. (b) This shows a 'near normal' joint with head falling away very slightly from the socket.(c) A dysplastic joint – note separation between head and socket. (d) Dysplasia with severe luxation of head out of the socket – note change in shape of both head and socket.

life in a crate which erodes his constitution and muscle tone. These 'evolved' breeds managed to make it through at least 2000 years without any of this but look what's happened in less than 100 years of man's 'concern' for his dog.

Stress is the number one killer in North America, as well as being the prime cause of numerous conditions in animals, and dogs in particular. Stress depletes the vitamin C in the body; if sufficient is not available, the reserves held in the collagen have to go, heralding softer muscles, looser hips and, surprisingly enough, HD. This could account for many hip problems caused by loose femoral heads in the acetabuli.

Why, you may ask, do some breeds and lines have more trouble than others? A Swedish vet, Dr-Stenn-Erik Olssen, observed that it was almost impossible to damage a Greyhound's hips. The Greyhound can be run or raced and, in the tradition of wheel-backed type dogs, finish smiling. Many regard this breed as having the best hips in the world. Dr Olssen bred one of these dogs to a line of German Shepherds with a bad record of HD. By careful selective breeding, he produced a dog with the physical appearance (phenotype) of a German Shepherd and the genotypical hips of a Greyhound. This dog was identifiable to the eye as a German Shepherd; however, under the disguise were the hips of a typical Greyhound.

Photo courtesy R. Vaillola

C.I.B. Balt Nord Fi Se No Est Lt Lv Ru Si Ch Bullcastle´s GoldenUelsiBora

Eventide

A medieval Saxon Baron was once sitting in his large hall having a feast with his friends, as Saxon Barons were wont to do, when a bird flew in from the dark, flitted briefly around the hall and disappeared again out into the inky night. Upon seeing this the Baron, who was usually considered a hard, insensitive person, reflected that the bird's action was a picture of life. We come from who knows where? We appear briefly on the scene of life, and then disappear just who knows where? In the millenniums of life our brief appearance is no longer than the bird's in the hall light.

The life span of a Bullmastiff is but a short 10 years or less, a possible 15% of the average human being's. When the time comes to fly back out into the night the way is not always clear; sometimes the exit is blocked by ignorance, insensitivity or, still worse, negligence.

Bullmastiffs are dogs with pride, loyalty, bravery and fidelity. Sometimes they do not know they are hurting or that they did not always walk the way they do today because of physical disabilities. Sometimes they just do not want to find the way out of the light even when they know it is high time. This is when you as a considerate owner must make the decision that will be hard to live with for many years after, but which must be faced. One thing you must remember is to let your Bullmastiff retain his pride and dignity to the very last. Be gentle and kind, but show him the way out of the hall into the darkness beyond in a way that he will thank you for, so that you can be content in your mind that it was the right time

Critics will say that some lines seem to be completely free of HD. It seems safe to say that, after the exhaustive activity of the Swedish army to remove HD from their dogs by severe and persistent culling, HD still appeared. The opinion at that time was that the HD was being controlled by a wild gene and could not be identified or subdued by man. Maybe the solution to finding this wild gene was always present depending on where the observer was looking and under whose guidance. Maybe the seekers were looking in the wrong place. Everyone was looking for a gene because they had been told to look for a gene. Maybe, just maybe, it was not the fault of the gene but of the environment. Such a hypothesis is hard to prove or disprove because of the money, facilities and size of cross-section needed for such testing. Maybe it's time to look at this problem from a different direction and examine new ideas about this subject which has eluded man up until now. It is always easier to cling to the side you know than strike out into deep water and the unknown but how else will the swimmer and this noble breed of Bullmastiffs survive? **One Titanic is enough!**